Frank Faulkner has spent all his life based in his native Northamptonshire. He served in both the Northamptonshire Regiment and Police Force. Retiring from the latter he found the freedom to pursue what he would have preferred to be doing all along. Travelling, especially by train and in Australia. He is still trying to retire.

TRUST ME-I'M YOUR TOUR MANAGER!
"A personal journey"

"Clay lies still, but blood's a rover;
Breath's a ware that will not keep.
Up, lad; when the journey's over
They'll be time enough to sleep."

Reveille by A.E. Houseman

Dedication

"For Christine who should have travelled this journey
with me."

Frank Faulkner

TRUST ME-I'M YOUR TOUR MANAGER!
"A personal journey"

AUSTIN MACAULEY
PUBLISHERS LTD.

A CIP catalogue record for this title is available from the British Library.

ISBN 978 14963 617 9

www.austinmacauley.com

First Published (2014)
Austin Macauley Publishers Ltd.
25 Canada Square
Canary Wharf
London
E14 5LB

Printed and bound in Great Britain

Acknowledgments

To Harriet
My love and inspiration, guide and minder
these last forty years

The Boss
For entrusting his customers to me

And the Grandkids
Georgie, Sage and Talfryn
who will continue the journey.

Contents

Chapter 1

Be Prepared!

"I don't want to worry you Frank."

"Try me, Mary."

"I've just flushed my false teeth down the sink!"

Given time, most situations can be rectified, but this occurred when the programme was already running late and we were disembarking from a Rhine Cruise boat at Cologne with little enough time to walk up to the nearby Railway Station.

And German trains leave on time.

Chapter 2

In The Beginning

I am unsure where my enthusiasm for travel came from. Certainly not from my early years.

I was born in a little thatched cottage in Duck Street, Rushden, one of the Boot and Shoe towns strung along the A6 through Northamptonshire. When away from my first bed, which was the wicker laundry basket, I suspect that my early journeys would only have been to visit many uncles, aunts and my grandparents, all of whom lived in the same small town.

The depression years of the '30s were hard times indeed for my parents and the reason, I was told, that I didn't acquire any brothers and sisters. My father, born in 1902, was fortunate in being too young for the First World War and too old for the Second when he joined the AFS (Auxiliary Fire Service) rather than Dad's Army of TV fame, although I'm not sure if he had a choice. His contribution to the war effort was to sleep under the billiard table at the Fire Station, in the next street, on one night a week and to continue 'Digging for Victory' on his large organic allotment, although 'Organic' was not in the vocabulary at that time. A great deal of my leisure time was spent helping out on the allotment when not wandering the local fields. The only sanction was to be home in time for meals.

The wartime years presented few opportunities to travel outside one's immediate area and if proof of that were needed it would be in several Sunday School prizes for 52 attendances in a year! Dad was a great walker and a Saturday or Sunday evening would often be spent walking "across the fields" to a nearby village which might have been Wymington, Chelveston or Irchester for a drink in a pub and a bus ride back.

There was no use of private cars during the war years and little for some time after. My parents never owned a car so when Uncle George acquired an ancient vehicle and occasionally took us all out "for a little ride round the block" this was a great excitement and could have aroused my early interest in travel.

I don't recall any interest in my daily school bus journey to Wellingborough but there was always a tinge of the exotic on a rare outing to Northampton market – with maybe a cup of tea and a sensible cake at the fume-filled Derngate Bus Station café. But the annual Sunday School outing – always to Wicksteed Park at Kettering – was a long and eagerly anticipated journey.

About this time I vaguely recall two really long-distance day expeditions with my mother to visit an aunt in Husbands Bosworth. Although only just over the border in Leicestershire it involved six train journeys: Rushden to Wellingborough, Wellingborough to Northampton, Northampton to North Kilworth and then a long walk to Husbands Bosworth. As this all had to be repeated to return home we could not have enjoyed much time at our destination.

I only recall one weekend away during these years, to an 'Uncle and Aunt' in Leicester. Most of my parents' friends were given relative status. I only know in retrospect that most were not related and I now have no avenue open to discover who these people were. But I do remember the exhilaration riding on the open front of a Leicester tram, which Uncle Alec drove.

One really long journey about which I have almost no memory would have been a holiday in Margate in 1939. The evidence for being there is provided by two fading photographs, one with me sitting on a very mangy stuffed lion and in another I'm holding hands with a vast panda – probably the same location, different props! It is difficult to separate what you are told about your childhood from personal memory but I seem to recall climbing aboard a train at Rushden station in the dark (for the long overnight journey to Margate?) Maybe it was just very early morning? Could this have stirred my yearning for travel?

Or maybe it could have been even earlier when I was taken to Rushden station in my pram in hopes of seeing the Rushden 'Gusher' which shuttled back and forth on the branch line to Wellingborough. And as this happened pretty irregularly there must have been disappointments.

But at age 10 my travelling days were to take off with a daily journey to Wellingborough Grammar School, physically and mentally far from the sheltered years at Rushden Newton Road Infant and Junior schools, which my mother also attended. A contemporary of hers at this school was the prolific Rushden author H.E. Bates from whose autobiography, "The Vanished World", I gain a lively picture of the Rushden in which they both grew up and yet had changed little by my childhood years.

Chapter 3

Baptism of Fire

"We'll start you with a simple trip," from the Boss of the Tour Operation to whom I'd offered my services. Orkney and Shetland! I'd never been to either and didn't see myself cast in the role of "Your experienced Tour Manager" [although in those days I was called a Courier] but after 30 years' Police experience in a variety of departments I felt I could continue to handle most situations with confidence.

No problems anticipated – all the passengers would be on the 10.30 a.m. train from Euston to Perth for the first night's stay. I had a list of their names and reserved seat numbers so I would be able to "Meet and Greet" all during the 8 hours on board, whether they joined at Euston or at subsequent stations. On our arrival at Perth the Station Hotel was a short walk across the station forecourt. On Day 2 we would take a train for the brief journey to Aberdeen where I would be met by the P+O shipping agent and transfer to the ship, on which the passengers would be their responsibility for the next three days.

Now I generally get on with most people but really didn't take enthusiastically to a spotty individual who introduced himself as a "Junior Travel Executive of Thomas Cook's". I think the feeling was probably reciprocated when I informed him that I used to be one of those but in my day I was called a Counter Clerk.

Several passengers were missing when the train pulled out of Euston. I found them all eventually – but not in their reserved seats because they preferred to sit somewhere else, usually at a window or facing the other direction. All 52 passengers, which was to be my biggest party ever, were on board by the time we reached Perth station and managed to walk across the forecourt to the hotel where I was greeted by, "Due to a computer fault the hotel is trebly overbooked!" and my party were not the first claimants. In these circumstances it is customary for the hotel to relocate you at their expense and, usually, add an upgrade, so after a quick cuppa we boarded a coach for the Dunblane Hydro – 25 miles back towards Edinburgh. OK so far, and a huge sigh of relief from "our Experienced Tour Manager" who, in the next 21 years, was only 'bumped' once more, and that in the quite amusing circumstances which come later.

After a relaxing swim in the Hydro pool and an enjoyable dinner and breakfast I found all the party already boarded on the coach which was to take us to Aberdeen – except two people – Junior Travel Executive and his wife whom I traced to a noisy altercation with the hotel manager, they having apparently locked themselves out of their room containing the lady's handbag, their cases already having been loaded on the coach. Neither their room key nor the master key, both assisted by my size 10 boot, could effect an entry and they were adamant that they would not leave the hotel without the handbag. Time was disappearing fast and our train would not wait for us, at which point I mentally recorded my First Rule of the successful Tour Manager, 'Get to the end of the Tour with the majority of the passengers!'

With great reluctance they joined the party on the coach after I had assured them that the hotel manager must eventually gain access to the room and he would then, at my suggestion, forward the handbag by the excellent Red Star parcel service to the shipping company at Aberdeen so it would be waiting for us when we disembarked on our return three days later.

Then they complained that they had missed their breakfast and what was I going to do about that? I telephoned the hotel at Perth, from where we were continuing our journey, and arranged for a cooked breakfast to be waiting for them when they arrived there. By that time they seemed to have lost their appetite but I believe that the breakfast wasn't wasted.

Our shipping agent was waiting for us with a bus at Aberdeen station and the party was quickly transferred to our floating hotel for the weekend where they would be in the care of the ship's crew, and regular announcements would leave them in no doubt what their mealtimes were and details of shore leave and excursion possibilities in both Orkney and Shetland.

Peace at last? No chance. I was regularly asked if the bag had been recovered, was it in Aberdeen, and would it be waiting for us? The owner and her husband became increasingly disturbed whilst the likely extraction from their credit cards increased by steep increments as did the possibility of loss and damage at the office premises for which the keys were carried.

Came Monday – and as usual, after the first of my many weekends in those wonderful islands, our ship reversed into Aberdeen harbour. There was increased agitation from both the handbag loser and her husband who were convinced that the bag would not be waiting for them.

They were right!

Real hysterics required significant restraint from several of the other passengers who had become pretty fed up with their behaviour over the weekend, to such an extent that they had been virtually ostracised and therefore directed all their whinges to me.

Our agent in Aberdeen had not received the Red Star package although calls to Dunblane confirmed that the bag had been recovered from the bedroom and dispatched soon after we had left; moreover confirmation of its receipt was not entered in the Aberdeen Red Star office registration book. The delivery man was "somewhere in Aberdeen".

It took a great deal of persuasion, part physical, to get a by-now near-demented woman on to our train at Aberdeen whilst I stood at the end of the platform looking out for a couple of scouts from the shipping office who were quartering Aberdeen for the Red Star delivery van.

2 minutes to departure. "You better get on if you're travelling," from the guard. Reluctantly I did so but hung out

of the very last window as the train started to move slowly south – at which point appeared a familiar figure, running, who caught up with the train and threw a Red Star package in through the window. Yes, the 'missing' handbag, complete with all its contents. Received with an almost total collapse and floods of tears from the loser – from whom no thanks.

That was my first and probably my worst trip in 21 years and with the largest party I was ever given. I felt I had acquitted myself well enough in my 'shepherd' role and could handle anything that came after. But even as I started my last trip, 21 years later, and looked back and thought I must have encountered every possible permutation of what could go wrong – I hadn't.

On my second, completely problem-free, trip with just a dozen passengers the Boss came along to "show me the ropes".

Chapter 4

Wheels – and a Bicycle Made for Two

At 10 I didn't own my own bicycle but occasionally borrowed Dad's heavy duty, single-speed, upright model on which I had learned to ride, after lowering the saddle. I remember, quite clearly, the place in Allen Road, Rushden where I first went solo. I'm not sure of the origin of this bike as it was painted in a distinctive shade of military olive drab, which caused me some anxiety when passing the many military establishments which proliferated during the war years, particularly just before D Day and where all their equipment and vehicles were painted in the identical colour.

Otherwise I borrowed a lady's 'Sit up and beg' from Uncle George, who lived in the next street and, with my friend Dave, explored local cross country footpaths and bridleways. It must sometimes have been returned in a pretty muddy state but I was never reprimanded by my favourite uncle.

Without a bicycle I was unable to reach swimming lessons from Wellingborough Grammar School at Wilby Lido (no luxury coach travel in those days). This was no great hardship as I was not enamoured of cold water outdoor pools (nor of swimming).

I didn't acquire my own wheels until I was 15, and working, although that was not achieved with initial parental approval. I was travelling to work at Kettering on 6 days a week and my weekly bus ticket of 10 shillings (50p) swallowed a large proportion of my meagre weekly pay of 25 shillings (£1.25p). I figured that if I could cycle the 22 mile return journey daily I could save that 10 shillings. I studied cycle catalogues assiduously and eventually settled on a Dawes Flambeau with a Caradice saddlebag which could be bought with nearly all my savings of £30. Parents not impressed. "Savings is Savings – not to be spent!" so I continued my daily bus journey for some time but they must have relented quite soon as by the middle of 1950 I was cycling to and from Kettering most days (except in very foul weather). But a condition of my purchase was that my notional weekly savings had to be returned to my savings account – so I was actually no better off, but fitter.

With decent wheels and much youthful energy my horizons expanded rapidly and regular excursions within and without the county were made – usually on my Thursday half-day off or on Sunday. I set myself a target of visiting every county adjacent to Northamptonshire, and as our long thin county was at that time surrounded by more counties than any other in the UK this involved some fairly long days out.

For my annual one-week holiday in 1950, Dave and I really decided to take off big time. My original YHA card records a cycle tour of southern England staying at Oxford, Winchester, Swanage, Cheddington, Gosport, Hannington and Jordans hostels. We liked early starts and that often involved performing an evening duty and then, in the morning, extracting our bikes from under mountains of others.

I'm not sure when or how the next idea occurred to us but in 1952 we splashed out on a second-hand tandem, for £5 each, whereupon our daily range increased considerably when we discovered that two energetic peddlers on one bike could cover a minimum of 100 miles a day with ease. Our tour that year was my first visit to North Wales and made a lasting impression on one from the fairly flat East Midlands. I don't remember us walking up the steepest hills but the very fast long downhill runs were exhilarating. One of my favourite hostels there, and a regular port of call on many other visits since, was Rowen, high up on the west side of the Conway valley. My visit there in 2010 was exactly 59 years to the date of my first stay! Wales has been my spiritual home ever since and I later became quite determined to live there one day.

My daily journeys to Kettering ended on November 5th 1951 when I started what was to be my employment for the next 31 years, (excepting 2 years of National Service). In retrospect I only remember that I became a Police Cadet because it would more than double my salary to £11 a month – unimagined wealth! It also meant that I was now only to work 5 days a week, and Wellingborough, where I was to be stationed, was a shorter distance to cycle each day. At that stage shift working also appeared to give free time for other activities on part of every day.

But winter cycling at 6 am for early shift had its detractions so it was back on the bus at 11d (5.5p) a day until that Eureka moment when I found that a daily return by train from Rushden to Wellingborough was only 10 1/2d (5.25p). And I really preferred the train journey, although it involved a much longer walk at both ends. Maybe somewhere here my lifelong love of train travel was starting to develop but it was hardly surprising that the branch line was later a victim of Beeching. I was often the only passenger on the train on both journeys.

Chapter 5

Some People!

The Company which I successfully represented for 21 years was originally formed to operate day excursions by chartered trains but, due mainly to British Railways losing interest in providing trains and in any case jacking up the cost, the business gradually developed into "Short Breaks by Rail" using scheduled train services and was, initially, mainly to Scotland.

For many years it operated in this niche market with considerable success, not least attracting railway employees and pensioners for whom the tours represented great value. They used their free or discounted travel facility and benefited from our bulk purchase of hotel accommodation and services. Accordingly the tours tended to attract older customers but people, unlike most coach passengers, still with enough energy to carry their own bags on and off trains, coaches and, later, planes plus the initiative to find their way to the start of the tour from the detailed itinerary provided.

Nevertheless, I was presented with a complete cross-section of the older population over the years.

It was usual to meet most passengers on their initial rail journey and brief them about their first evening and next day activities and timings. Otherwise we all met over dinner at the hotel – very occasionally some failed to show up at this time, sometimes because of late running rail services. Some didn't show up at all! There could be challenging problems straight away – like the elderly gent I met in his seat on a Eurostar heading for two changes of train before our arrival at Frankfurt. He informed me that he needed a wheelchair, hadn't brought one and neither had the Company been warned of his need! With quite sharp connections in Brussels and Cologne this required a lot of fast and decisive activity on the part of the Tour Manager whose French and German, is, to say the least, basic – but we survived. Our first objective was a Rhine Cruise vessel moored at Frankfurt and, once loaded, our passenger remained on board for the next four days, thankfully declining all shore excursions. With notice of his requirement the return journey could be planned with less drama.

I only encountered two other wheelchair passengers in my travels. One gentleman, accompanied by his wife, was a joy to have in tow. She had wisely consulted the company who referred her to me and we had a long discussion of the possibilities on the whole range of our tours before deciding which would be the most suitable.

The other, a Doctor of what discipline I know not, was a vast lady who assured us that her accompanying friend could cope. Friend turned out to be an elderly and very slight lady incapable of managing the wheelchair on the level, and pushing up the steep ramp on to our ferry to Shetland was out of the question. Despite every kindness and consideration by the ship's crew and me she remained totally demanding and aggressive throughout, much to the embarrassment of the friend and other members of the party who offered help (just once!).

Sometimes friends decided to take a holiday together after some years apart. This in itself led to some shocks to the parties involved. One quite large tour, staying in fully booked hotels, included two ladies who had not met for many years since one had emigrated to Australia. Not unusually for friends, and to save the singles supplement, they booked to share a twin room. After one night the Australian lady demanded to move to a single room – having discovered that in the intervening years her 'friend' had become an almost-chain smoker greatly to the detriment of her health and comfort. For the next few nights single rooms there were none. The situation was resolved by the Tour Manager giving up his single room for the rest of the tour – and for those who are ahead of me at this stage, NO, I didn't move in with the smoker but occupied a series of the usual very grotty staff rooms and linen cupboards at subsequent hotels.

Chapter 6

Lost Passenger Award

Proudly displayed amongst my silver is my Lost Passenger Award which brings back memories of a week of great anxiety when a passenger I was sure I had seen board a train with the party at Glasgow Central station was missing when we arrived at Ardrossan Harbour to embark on a CalMac ferry for Arran.

All but one boarded the ferry with me going through various contingency plans to re-unite her with the party should she turn up elsewhere and seek help. It was possible that she had alighted at a different Ardrossan station. But show up she singularly failed to do, either on that day or during the following two days. The Office was of course alerted and they initiated enquiries at her home address. Sadly, but I suspect not untypically, neither immediate neighbour knew anything about her nor whether she had any local family. She was reported as a Missing Person to various Scottish Police forces.

I had to explain our loss to the party, one of whom said, "I think I saw her at the platform," and she had asked, "Where is the Station?" Having worked with old people for Age Concern this question immediately rang a bell as the comment of someone with a problem.

By Day 3 we had reached Oban and I checked in at the Police Station. By strange and good fortune my description of the lady was overheard by a passing officer who said that he had just spoken to her – she had approached him in the street and, showing a hotel key fob, declared that she had forgotten where the hotel was.

We both went to the hotel and there was my Lost Passenger. I suggested that she might like to re-join the party but she was quite adamant that she was not with a party and was, in any case, going home tomorrow. I really had no option but to let her.

The fallout from this incident was an increasingly acrimonious correspondence from her son claiming a refund of fare and significant damages for various reasons. "Mother was on an escorted tour and should not have been abandoned!" This continued for some time until my boss's wife telephoned the son but instead spoke to his wife who confessed that they knew that Mum was unwell but didn't realise quite how badly. Presumably realising that the cat was now well and truly out of the bag the correspondent rested his attacks.

Fortunately on this tour I was accompanied by a trainee tour manager, a mature man of common sense who needed very little instruction to keep the show on the road whilst I was otherwise engaged. Fred was a great comfort and support and virtually ran the tour, freeing me to co-ordinate my efforts and enquiries in the search.

Over the years I was sometimes confronted by obviously less-able passengers but with a little warning they could be kept under closer watch and others in the party invariably rallied round to assist the 'shepherd'.

Generally speaking I finished few tours with unresolved problems but the ones which really hurt were from the 'smiling assassins' who assured you that they had thoroughly enjoyed their holiday and then wrote letters of complaint, sometimes many weeks later. In the early days complaints were virtually unheard of but over the years and with media encouragement complaints became more frequent and usually pettier. The Boss was one of the world's superb letter writers and many correspondents must soon have realised that they were on to a loser pursuing an unjustified complaint – especially if they included Biblical quotations.

I was always at pains to emphasise that most problems could be, and usually were, resolvable at the time, quoting such examples as a complaint of a dirty thumb mark on a dinner plate made six weeks afterwards or of no bulb in a bedside light. I am at a loss to understand what some complainants hoped to gain. Actual Value for Money rarely featured in these correspondences.

And who would book a tour of the Highlands and then complain that "We just rode about looking at mountains!"

The highlight of a tour to the Western Isles was a boat excursion from Iona to Fingal's Cave on the island of Staffa, but achieved on about only half the tours due to very unpredictable sea conditions which couldn't be anticipated a year in advance when the brochure was written. Our local boatman was a vastly experienced skipper in these waters and it was, of course, his absolute decision as to whether we sailed, or landed, or not.

The passengers were naturally disappointed when the decision was negative and it was sometimes difficult for them to appreciate, when weather and sea conditions were good at the point of embarkation.

This was occasionally a cause for a written complaint. In quick succession we received, "I was in the Navy for many years and we should have sailed!" followed by, "I was in the Navy for many years and we should never have sailed in those conditions!" (We did have a few "interesting" trips!). The writer of letter 1 was simply sent a copy of Letter 2 and vice versa.

End of correspondence.

Chapter 7

So What is a Tour Manager?

Originally I was called a Courier, but that word came to be associated with the enthusiastic drivers of white vans (and I did that too!) and Motor Cycle messengers driving willy-nilly over pavements and insinuating themselves between cars and lorries the moment that traffic stopped moving. Tour Manager came to us, surprise, surprise, from the States where no tour was complete without one.

A Tour Manager is not a guide, more of a shepherd, to ensure that his tour runs smoothly and that, when necessary, passengers' concerns are met. Good briefing will normally ensure the former and avoid the latter. Some upper crust tours have both a Tour Manager and a guide (the Travel Graduate variety have often failed to impress me) in addition to a driver, all adding to the dubious economics of running a tour at a profit. The guide will normally point out matters of interest in view and in the locality – where there is only a Tour Manager he/she will combine this role. Some say too little to create and maintain an interest, some say much too much. You can normally judge if the quantity is about right by the number of sleeping heads you see in the interior rear view mirror, especially after lunch.

I was initially just a Courier to parties travelling by train to our first night destination and thereafter we used local coaches. When booking a coach we often specified a particular driver who was known to the Company, many of whom shared a knowledge and enthusiasm for their local area but who tended to become less knowledgeable when further from their base. Some were quite excellent and took a pride in disseminating an interesting commentary. I was usually monitoring their performance for future bookings. From time to time we were provided with drivers who, although perfectly competent to drive, had either no interest in commentating or whose offering was a litany of urban myths, jokes, sometimes of dubious quality, or a tirade against other motorists. This, inevitably, led to complaints.

On one of my early tours I was amazed to hear a driver telling us that a certain plant, which was covering the stone walls of the Bridge over the Atlantic to Seil Island in Western Scotland in dramatic and colourful profusion, grew "nowhere else in the world!"

Rubbish! – Erinus alpinus grows almost anywhere, including in my garden.

There was also an increasing awareness that they really should not be distracted by commentating when driving a very large vehicle, sometimes in heavy traffic, and prosecutions in some areas led to a reluctance on the part of some drivers to do so.

The worst drivers were those who, given a mike, thought they were God's gift to the entertainment business. The very best one I ever encountered had a passionate interest in his island of Skye and was fluent in English, Gaelic, Scots Doric and Mandarin.

Having thoroughly researched every trip before departure, either from serious guide books, and later also from the Internet, I soon came to the conclusion that I could do better than most drivers. I also felt that I should be in a position to answer any sensible queries from my passengers, although beyond my remit and, early on, armed myself with the authoritative Blue Guide to Scotland – my 50-year old knowledge from geography at school, where remembered, being largely out of date.

My passengers came as a group of mixed ages, mixed interests and mixed abilities and I took great care to try and provide a commentary on a fairly broad spectrum. About 15 minutes each hour is quite long enough to bend their ears and I sometimes had to rein myself in when covering a subject of particular personal interest.

Material provided by local Tourist Information Centres

was often little more than inducements to spend lotsamoney locally – that's what they exist for – coupled with a dearth of solid general information. Some were quite unable to answer simple local questions.

A situation occurred on one tour when it became obvious to me that I was being tested by a couple of passengers. It was soon evident from their queries that they were also in possession of a Blue Guide. This ended when I referred them to the page number in their book where the answer was found. I simply said, "The answer is at the bottom of the page in the book from which you are asking the questions." Applause from other passengers, who were getting thoroughly fed up by a pair of apparent know-alls who were monopolising my attention,

Dear old Billy was my driver for most of my 34 visits to Orkney and most passengers found his broad Orcadian accent quite difficult to understand. His local knowledge and enthusiasm were second to none. To our mutual amusement we did a class double act with me providing the English subtitles. Billy knew everyone on Orkney (and they all knew him!) – so when a tour passenger wished to try and find a local acquaintance with whom he had lost contact, Billy was the man to ask. Within minutes he was traced to his weekend shack on the adjacent island of Hoy which we were due to visit the following day, when the pair were re-united.

Magnus, the most complete driver in Shetland, never failed to ensure rapt attention from every passenger, with a perfect balance of the local knowledge which only an enthusiastic native could give, leavened by subtle humour. We always requested Magnus – but so did other companies and we occasionally had to settle for the second team.

Whilst to a certain degree a repeat tour could lead to a largely repeated, if enhanced, commentary I found that a spontaneous performance, based on a sound local knowledge in which conditions could vary considerably, was preferable. There can be nothing more frustrating than listening to an enthusiastic catalogue of things that can't be seen. I was also very aware that from my 'suicide seat' beside the driver my view was much superior to that of most of the passengers in the comfy but high-backed seats of modern coaches.

One little stunt which I did, however, repeat with appreciation was not disclosing the dramatic location of the Isle of Barra hotel. In Spring and Autumn, after the ferry crossing from Lochboisdale, we usually arrived after dark and I ensured that the bedroom curtains would be closed. Waking the following morning revealed that we were virtually on the beach of the beautiful Halaman Bay, often with one set of footprints leading away across the magnificent white sand. (No prizes for guessing.)

This was a hotel that lost the excellent reputation of many years on a change of ownership for a short period. That reputation was difficult to claw back but this has been achieved by the current family owners.

Whilst mobile phones were not in general use in my early days as a Tour Manager they became increasingly common to the situation where virtually every passenger was in possession of one. I always circulated my mobile number and it did come in very useful on a couple of occasions when passengers became slightly lost.

And if your TM occasionally seems a bit weary do remember that he's either on duty or on call to his party from the moment he leaves home until he shuts the door behind him on his return.

Chapter 8

Entry into the Travel Business

Leaving Wellingborough Grammar School with a School Certificate described in a reference by the Headmaster as "a strong result for a 15-year old" (I was actually 14!) I really had no idea what direction I wanted to pursue – in fact I didn't discover that until I retired. Careers counselling was then unheard of but no-one in my class left school without a job! A school pal, Gus Manning, started work with a Travel Agency. We kept in touch after our schooldays and he seemed to be doing something interesting at the Wellingborough office of Frames' Tours – I applied for an interview at the Kettering branch of the same company and started work there as a Counter Clerk on January 1st (which was not then a Bank Holiday) in 1950.

This involved 5 1/2 long days when including the hour-long bus journey at each end of the day (or Thursday half-day). The days were no shorter when I acquired a smart lightweight bike for my daily journeys but the 20 miles daily got me pretty fit for my cycling holidays of the next few years.

Long before wide-bodied jets and package holidays the main business of Travel Agents was the sale of railway tickets and our office in Market Street, Kettering, was backed by a vast rack of the small card Edmondson tickets then issued. My first job daily was to change the date stamp for these tickets, a task which inevitably left my hands covered with indelible ink! Thereafter I was responsible for re-aligning the many rail excursion leaflets displayed on a board outside the door (which was a favourite calling point for the local dogs) and tidying miscellaneous other brochures lining the wall below the rail ticket racks, before eventually dealing with customers. That meant mainly consulting timetables and selling railway tickets – a crash course in UK geography.

1950 was a Passion Play year. The only package we sold was Oberammergau to which we despatched a party from the local Catholic School for the great sum of about £15 per head to include rail and ferry fares, accommodation, play tickets and the teachers' 'free' fares. Toying with an increasing desire to travel I couldn't overlook the fact that even this quite modest tour would consume nearly 3 months of my salary – or years of what was left of it after paying my living expenses. Anyway, local exploration on my newly-acquired bike satisfied my travel for those years.

In my two years at the Travel Agency we did not sell a single air ticket – although we had all the timetables – which I read avidly – crash course in world geography. I particularly remember BEA Highland Division flights to a place called Barra where the landing was *tide-dependent. Remarking to the manager that I didn't realise that BEA still flew seaplanes I was put down with the equivalent of, "Stupid boy – the plane lands on the beach NOT the SEA!" It still does, but it was to be 40 years before I actually saw this happening – on the only runway washed twice a day. I have yet to enjoy the flight but I will this year thanks to a thoughtful and exciting present from my wife.

The weekly task causing unbelievable problems and head-scratching was the Monday morning balancing, on a vast white form, of the previous week's sales of railway tickets against the tickets remaining and cash received, On a good day this could take a few hours, on a bad day it might extend into Tuesday. This was before the days of calculators being in general use, and many re-runs on huge columns of figures were sometime made before a correct balance was achieved.

It being so soon after WWII and the return to North America of many British GI Brides there was considerable demand from parents to visit them, and maybe see their grandkids for the first time. To that end we did reserve many passengers on the transatlantic liners of many steamship companies, particularly for members of Canuspa (Canadian and US parents association). The fare was £59 – with a 3-year waiting list.

Our other major business was the reservation of tickets for London theatres as agents for TTM – Theatre Tickets and Messengers. It's hard to recall that few people had a telephone in their home and mobiles were not yet invented. We held seating plans of all the London theatres and would make telephone reservations (London Temple Bar 1023) with customers giving Yes or No to the seat options proffered, and then paying for the seats plus the telephone call . . . usually buying a train ticket as well.

Interval I – National Service

After a very short back and sides I presented myself with many others at Quebec (later Simpson) Barracks in Northampton on 5.3.53 (a date indelibly imprinted on my mind) for what seemed an interminable prospect away from our homes and girlfriends.

In what I later came to realise was normal perverse military procedure, and having volunteered for the RAF, I found myself in the Infantry,

In a totally new and confusing environment, being chased, harassed, abused and sworn at by "thick regulars" I probably wasn't the only person in my barrack room who cried himself to sleep that first night.

After another day of being chased around and sworn at by our NCOs whose IQs would have difficulty in reaching double figures I don't suppose many of us looked forward to this prospect for the next two years (minus one day – we noted!).

We were given the option to sign on for a 3-year engagement rather than the standard period of 2 years for National Service, the inducements being that our 4 shillings (20p) a day pay would double and we would get weekend leave straight away. The alternative was no leave for six weeks. Another inducement was that we would be transferred straight away to a Regiment then serving in the plum posting of Trieste whilst the 2 year National Servicemen were heading for Korea.

I hardly need tell any ex-National Servicemen that what actually happened was that the regular transferees headed straight for Korea whilst the others lived well on 4 bob a day on an ace posting to Wuppertal in Germany.

Before the end of my first two weeks of incarceration I was transferred to Gibraltar Barracks in Bury St Edmunds – which brought me weekend leave straight away and the weekly prospect of hitching home along what was then the A45. Although there were few cars and trucks in 1953 most would give servicemen in uniform a lift and this journey was completed effortlessly for a few months. When occasionally in funds I would sometimes make the return journey on Sunday evenings by train via Bedford and Cambridge.

A posting to Eaton Hall near Chester followed, with a regular long train journey in prospect. This opened new horizons and I was able to renew my acquaintance with North Wales, albeit at a distance from serious mountains, with Sunday rail excursions along the North Wales coast. I was also fascinated to find evidence of the derelict narrow-gauge railway line which formerly delivered the Duke of Westminster's supplies to his country seat of Eaton Hall from Chester station. When this posting ended I ricocheted between Bury St Edmunds and Northampton by train for some weeks, but eventually caught up the boys I had joined up with, in Wuppertal.

It was on the journey to Wuppertal that I first encountered a probable nudge towards a latent travel interest. We travelled across the North Sea from Harwich on the infamous troopship 'Vienna' followed by a long international train journey to Wuppertal. We were fed splendid meals on the train which certainly kick-started my lifelong pleasure of meals on (steel) wheels. Sadly this possibility has almost disappeared from British railway journeys.

The German barracks there were unbelievably comfortable with central heating and the first double glazing I had ever seen, and couldn't have been more different from the Victorian barracks in Bury St Edmunds and other places in the UK.

In retrospect I find it humbling that so soon after the end of WWII the inhabitants of a city almost destroyed by Bomber Command should extend a warm hand of friendship to British servicemen. Taking advantage of a general invitation I was able to visit a German family in Wuppertal and their relations in the country in their homes most weekends and on my first Christmas... away from home, parents and girlfriend. To reach their home I travelled by tram, then on the famous "Danglebahn" – the train suspended from wheels above the coaches on a steel framework – through the city above the River Wupper. On some weekends when it was closed for maintenance I used a local ancient steam train with short rattling 4-wheel coaches with wooden seats. Interest in modes of train travel was growing.

Interval II – National Service II

The Northamptonshire Regiment was posted from Germany to
Korea before the advent of the wide-bodied jet. This involved
a very long sea voyage by troopship. I discovered that I was a
Good Sailor and didn't fall victim to the awful scourge of sea
sickness. I was therefore glad to be in the top bunk of three.

I travelled with the small advance party on the troopship 'Empire Fowey' soon after the ill-fated 'Empire Windrush', which caught fire and sank in the Mediterranean in 1954, although with no loss of life. After a roughish crossing of the Bay of Biscay I recall a distant vision of Lisbon before Gibraltar, our first port of call. I didn't go ashore: maybe there was no shore leave – possibly I was on duty, with others, guarding the ship. I discovered that cruising in the Med in summer was rather pleasant, even on a troopship. The complete units on board, with their full complement of supervisory ranks, were kept busy training – in those useless tasks invented to keep soldiers occupied. Small parties, like the one in which I was travelling, were more or less left to their own military devices, i.e. look busy, carry a clipboard and no one will grab you for any duties. We sailed gently on to Malta and Port Said with no shore leave at the latter for me (I had obviously been rumbled) and I have a memory of the Suez Canal and distant views of pyramids in pauses between swabbing the decks – a pleasant enough task in the sunshine. British soldiers, ashore, exhorted us to, "Get yer knees brown!" as we sailed past.

Aden brought shore leave in the sort of heat most of us had not encountered before and it was a relief to get back aboard until assailed by the full force of a very rough Indian Ocean. The reward was a few hours ashore in steamy Colombo. The weeks (towards demob) were ticking away pleasantly enough and a further break in Singapore was followed by the long haul to Hong Kong for more leave in an acutely-fascinating environment. We next pulled into somewhere in southern Japan, about which I remember absolutely nothing. Maybe it was just a refuelling stop before the short trip across the Korea Strait to our final destination, Pusan in South Korea. This was 1954 and an armistice between the warring parts of Korea was in place (and still is 60 years later). Nevertheless, as we disembarked, we were greeted by a huge black American soldier with a tray hanging on a cord round his neck from which he dispensed United Nations medals (blue and white stripes aka 'butchers' aprons') to the landing troops. An

American army band played, "If I knew you were coming I'd have baked a cake!" Not quite a Buckingham Palace Investiture!

After a few days in a tented transit camp we boarded a steam train heading north to Seoul and all I recall seeing were endless rice paddies, wall-to-wall – a far cry from the modern industrial powerhouse that is South Korea. Army lorries took us forward to Teal Bridge camp, by the River Imjim, where the regiment was to take over from the Royal Warwickshires (who forever wallow in the glory of their most famous soldier, Monty). Living under canvas was quite acceptable in the warm autumn conditions until the monsoon struck and life underfoot became a constant choice between muddy water and watery mud. The monsoon ditches soon became waterlogged to overflowing and battalions of green and red frogs joined our living quarters.

These conditions were not destined to last for long and almost overnight winter arrived with a vengeance, when the water bowsers, collecting supplies from the Imjim, were superseded by three-ton trucks carrying blocks of ice. We were well equipped with clothing to survive in the intense cold but also mindful of the acute discomfort endured by the troops in the early days of the Korean War who were not so well clothed. And they were fighting a war against a determined enemy.

In the rarified atmosphere of the Battalion Orderly Room time passed quickly enough. No 1 grandson is disappointed to learn that as a soldier his granddad drove a typewriter and didn't actually shoot anyone! Then came a bonus of R+R (Rest and Recuperation) leave in Tokyo. Looking back to the crowded and bustling city it then was, it is difficult to imagine just how it appears today – I never had any wish to re-visit. Having spent most of my saved pay on a 21st birthday present for my girlfriend (something for the bottom drawer) my R+R comprised mainly the free tours included in the package. Most troops returning from R+R in Tokyo rejoined their units completely exhausted!

None too soon it was time to retrace the long cruise

homewards with a shipload of "days-to-do" National Servicemen not really amenable to anything other than acquiring a decent suntan.

Chapter 9

30 Years in a Nutshell

My ability to travel was significantly reduced in the early years of raising a family. One day off in seven and 50-hour weeks on shifts left little time, energy or cash for travel so our two-week holidays were largely spent in caravans at a variety of East Coast seaside towns.

We eventually expanded our horizons to Devon and Cornwall via the notorious Exeter Bypass – before the M25 this held the title of the country's biggest car park. We even travelled as far as the Channel Islands, initially by ferry from Weymouth where we held our breath as we watched our mini, suspended in a large net, drop into the hold of the ferry. Later visits were by air. These holidays were only of 1 or 2 weeks' duration – the remaining 50 weeks of the year being spent in and around Northamptonshire.

Work was generating an increasing amount of travel within the county. As one of 3 Police Scene of Crime Officers I reinforced an already-intimate knowledge of my county and covered many miles visiting both Scenes of Crime and Road Accidents in our long county, lying astride the A43 from south to north and crossed by many major road, rail and canal traffic corridors.

Promotion meant a return to shift working with its inevitable exhaustion and toll on my constitution but a later transfer to a training department again involved travelling around the county and I said goodbye to shift working for ever with immense benefit to my health and temper.

After other county-wide responsibilities in the Force I completed my Police career on secondment to a Home Office Scientific Research and Development Branch which is where my mileage, by road, rail and air expanded exponentially. The liaison role between the Home Office and provincial Forces involved travelling widely throughout the UK, initially by car, to conferences, lectures and to most Police Forces.

After a year or so I tentatively started using trains and significantly reduced the unproductive hours spent behind a wheel. It renewed my affection for train travel in an era when many long-distance trains also offered superb food, impeccably served by long-serving professional stewards. Sadly those days are but a memory for rail travellers.

Before the advent of mobile phones – yes, I go back that far – every First Class coach was a 'quiet coach' and I found I could arrive at meetings in the strong position of having read my briefing or lecture notes.

By this time we had also discovered the then-unspoiled Greek Islands for holidays. Friends found it hard to believe that we could exchange our frenetic lifestyle for 2 or 3 weeks with a pile of books, on a beach, turning over at half-hour intervals. Melanoma has yet to kick in.

Retirement, of a sort, continued my exposure to regular commuting by long-distance train. I was appointed Curator to the Royal Welch Fusiliers Regimental Museum within Caernarfon Castle but, having recently moved into a bungalow and large garden of our own design in Northamptonshire, we were reluctant to move out so soon. So for over two years I commuted on the Irish Mail between Rugby and Bangor for periods of about ten days with four days back at home to attack the garden. But even in retirement the attractions of what some considered a high profile/glamorous job began to pall when a back-of-envelope calculation revealed that we would actually be better off financially if I gave up work which involved owning two cars, two homes and the expense of travelling between them.

It didn't help that I shared an office with an assistant whose wife was supposed not to know that he smoked – so he consumed 60 a day at work! That was over 20 years ago. As I still enjoy good health I'm not convinced by reports of the effects of passive smoke but neither did I enjoy being kippered daily. I was dined out in great splendour and resumed living full-time in Northamptonshire.

Temporarily grounded but seeking further travelling opportunities I answered a plea from the Ambulance service: "Drivers wanted for patient conveyance." When they had checked my CV, refs and car insurance my initial journey was to Addenbrooks Hospital in Cambridge. This was the first of many occasions travelling with people in the close confines of a car who were coming to terms, or not, with terminal illnesses and who often seemed anxious to open their hearts. I hope I developed into a good listener.

Most journeys were local with occasional forays to most London hospitals, to Oxford regularly and to adjacent counties. They introduced me to many lovely people. One lady discovered my passion for bread pudding and there was always one waiting for me when I collected her for regular appointments – in fact she specifically requested me as her driver.

With patients sometimes in wheelchairs and often of limited mobility, ambulance cars were normally afforded the privilege of parking in spaces reserved for ambulances – except at Leicester! I was approached by a real little jobsworth, breathing fire and smoke and shouting, "You can't park there!" I explained that I was an ambulance car driver and had a very immobile patient whose wheelchair I was just extracting from my boot. "Where are you from?" he shouted – "Northampton" – I replied. The effect on this little uniformed man was truly dramatic – banging on the roof of my car for added emphasis for each word, he shouted, "We don't even allow FOREIGN ambulances to park in here!" I ignored him totally, locked my car and wheeled my patient into the hospital. By the time I returned to my car he was almost in a state of apoplexy, loudly enumerating the shortcomings of FOREIGN ambulances, ambulance cars and their drivers.

I always took a patient's own wheelchair, if possible, having learned the First Rule of hospital wheelchairs. If, by some rare good fortune, a wheelchair was immediately visible at the hospital entrance there was a more than even chance that it had flat tyres. Rule 2 was that most wheelchairs seemed to be about one inch wider than the average single hospital door and Rule 3 ensured that those doors would open against you.

I became very much aware of attitudes towards treatment, with some patients fully appreciating their hospital care and working hard towards recovery through physiotherapy and others who were never going to make it – being life's persistent moaners and repudiating all proffered help.

Sadly, these trips came to an end with a change of policy by the ambulance service. For some years my journeys were on an almost completely ad hoc call out system – they then decided that they needed to know my availability for a month ahead. Whilst I could usually provide this information there developed a sequence of months when I was called out to my inconvenience on days I had not offered while spending others confined to home. They seemed not to appreciate this – we parted company.

Looking for further travel opportunities I purchased a Rail Rover ticket for unlimited travel to, from, and on the Great Little Trains of Wales.

The following year the Company from whom I had purchased this ticket sent me their brochure for their Escorted Tours by Rail. Its receipt was one of those defining moments. I was not unused to dealing with the public in all its guises and felt that after 30 years as a copper I could manage guiding a flock around an itinerary – and get my travel free.

The rest, as they say, is history.

Chapter 10

Hotels (various – variable, very)

I am greeted at the largest hotel we ever and regularly used. Being a Station Hotel it was ideal for parties arriving by train and, despite its size and under several owners during this period, it seemed to maintain a high acceptable standard especially on this occasion, our first visit after a £20 million refit.

"Hello, Frank – we've got lots of empty rooms but as the computer is 'down' I'm afraid we can't tell you which they are!"

(Any shortage of rooms anywhere was invariably blamed on "computer problems.")

"OK, lend me a master key and a member of staff."

"What are you going to do?"

"What your cleaning staff do every day – bang on doors, wait a bit, and if no reply, enter. If vacant – park some of my party and update the computer when it gets better!"

"How will you know where they are?"

"Pencil and paper."

Unsurprisingly, common sense did not prevail and after a Management meeting the hotel stood an expensive meal to a large party who would much rather have got into a room for a refresh after a long day.

Working to a small brochure it was inevitable that after a couple of years repeat trips were made to increasingly familiar locations. This gives the Tour Manager the opportunity to learn his ground and local highlights and make useful contacts with the Company's service providers in that area.

This can be mutually advantageous when a hotel will give the party of a known and reliable Tour Manager a good choice of rooms and acceptable meal times.

When heavily booked, most hotels cannot feed all their guests at one sitting and some negotiation usually ensues to try and agree mutually-acceptable party timings. If you miss the favoured 7 o'clock service 6 is usually too early for most diners and 8 too late.

I was sometimes grateful to hotel management for shuffling around passengers from allocated rooms when, for whatever reason, they asked to change... to a room not adjacent to the dustbins or early morning deliveries to the kitchen back door... when those rooms were not, as usual, reserved for the Tour Manager/Coach Driver.

The whole standard of a hotel is often set by its owners and particularly by its manager. Both can change overnight without warning. Walking into a regularly-used station hotel one evening I immediately sensed bad vibes. Half the rooms had been let to the Social Services and our visit co-incided with the annual disco for the 'residents and friends'. By about 3 a.m. things were definitely hotting up, with the local Fire Brigade running through the corridors and into bedrooms looking for access to the roof from where a man was threatening to jump.

We didn't stay there again although the next change of ownership shortly after soon re-established the original standards but, by then, they had lost our custom.

Multiple Stars are no guarantee that a hotel offers a high standard of food, staffing and accommodation. The very best hotel we ever used had a lowly 2-star grading but superb staff, immaculate rooms, mostly with a sea view, and food to die for. Their weekend smorgasbord regularly drew gasps of wonder and appreciation from diners who often rushed back to their rooms for a camera to record this banquet. An additional star was never going to be awarded to this hotel, with no lift to all floors and no night porter.

Generally speaking if the grub was good there would be few complaints, even about fairly obvious shortcomings. Such a place in the Western Isles was inevitably christened Fawlty Towers by guests, who overlooked facilities which probably didn't even merit a single Star but offered superb and generous individually-cooked meals and a cosy bar where friendly locals gathered to sip their dram in front of a roaring fire.

As a Company we avoided Nouvelle Cuisine like the plague but it suddenly appeared with a new chef at the dining tables of one of our regular stops. Half a dozen courses of exquisitely beautiful but miniscule offerings, to a party largely consisting of ex-Railwaymen and their partners, were rejected with disdain. I took most of them out after Dinner and we enjoyed a Chinese and a pint.

Out of the blue one of the best and most reliable establishments suddenly lost all credibility after the appointment of a new manager. Meals were a complete disaster in seating, planning and quality of service and the party was understandably unhappy. My usual de-briefing report resulted in one manager looking for a new job and an almost complete change of staff under a trusted manager from the same chain.

Chapter 11

Hijacked – Over the Sea to Skye

Having presumably acquitted myself favourably on my first two tours a further pair was offered the next year.

The Isle of Skye tour always booked well but on the following occasion, in persistent rain and low cloud, Skye confirmed its reputation as 'The Misty Isle!' On these days the passengers might be excused for thinking that Skye was flat. Day 1 – magic – a journey along the 'World's most scenic railway line' to Kyle of Lochalsh and an excellent meal at an expensively-refurbished hotel there. Before the Skye Bridge was opened the CalMac ferry, from the front door of the hotel to Kyleakin on Skye, was always an attractive and interesting start to the day but as we approached our lunch stop on this occasion the weather rapidly deteriorated with only the merest suggestion of the first hundred feet of the normally spectacular Cuillin mountain range visible.

Before the days when the extensive coach and bus park was constructed at Portree the coach was simply parked on the main square until required again. The customers scuttled off in a near-gale to find their choice of refreshment. I noticed that our driver, Old (as opposed to Young) Kenny, showed no intention to lock the vehicle, on which, I had assured my passengers, their possessions would be safe. But Kenny was quite adamant it would be OK. "Nae problems up here, laddie!"

At the appointed return hour both Kenny and myself returned to the bus stance at the same moment. There was a pathetic gaggle of our folks trying to shelter from the cold blustery rain – but of our vehicle there was no sign! We did, however, notice another bus from the same company, destination "Uig", containing a few passengers but didn't give it another thought. After a quick search of the area a visit to the nearby bus depot revealed that a new driver had left some time previously to walk to the square and collect the service bus for Uig.

No prizes for guessing which one he had taken – NOT the one signed 'Uig' with passengers, but the empty one with lots of scattered baggage and possessions marked 'Private Hire'.

Kenny and I grabbed a taxi and headed for Uig but our bus was nearly there by the time we caught up with it – we had little choice but to allow it to drop and collect passengers from the Uig ferry there and perform a service run back to Portree where our people had been lodged (at Company expense of course) in a nearby hostelry with a warming dram of their choice. I must admit that they all took it in good part. Even Old Kenny was as near to an expletive as I ever heard from a practising and devout member of the "Wee Frees", who would sometimes offer up a prayer for a safe journey or even sing a hymn whilst at the wheel. There were many more trips with Kenny – but I noticed that thereafter he always locked the coach.

Trips to Skye bring to mind a visit to a well-known tourist honeypot on the island. It failed dismally to reach all its enthusiastically-advertised features and facilities. On departure I was handed an Evaluation Form and asked to complete it fully and truthfully. "This is the only way in which we can improve our service to you!" As a result of completing the form, 'fully and truthfully' the Boss soon received a smoking letter: "Mr Faulkner is permanently banned from visiting this establishment!" So much for truth.

Portree Square was also the scene of what appeared another potential disaster when an elderly man in the party tripped and fell as he neared the bus. He sat up, dazed, with blood pouring down his face and chest.

We were on a deadline, of course, and ferries don't wait, even for a booked coach and large party. I quickly parked the very shocked and blood-stained man in the local hospital, together with his wife and son who declined to leave him there alone, and we hurried away just in time to catch our ferry to

Lochmaddy on North Uist. I left them with a handful of Company travel vouchers with which they would be able to purchase tickets to follow us – if they were able – or to return home if not. They caught up with us the following day – in very good spirits – a very small plaster over one eye covering the source of the flood of the previous day.

In retrospect Skye seems to have been the scene of several of my potential problems over the years; likewise for a colleague, also heading for her ferry, confronted by an unplanned delay. All our coach travel was No Smoking, even before this became mandatory, but that does result in serious smokers, and often the driver, requesting a fag break, outside the vehicle. Such a request was made by a lady desperate for her fix. Despite really adverse weather and a serious warning about conditions underfoot she stepped off the coach, lighting up as she went, tripped and broke her ankle. Paramedics, more delay and another just-in-time ferry achieved. It's always good and usually planned, to have a few minutes in hand!

Question: Would you think it possible, as a passenger, to fail to notice the arrival of the small Skye ferry on the opposite shore, after a 10-minute journey, when that arrival was heralded by the clanking of the ramp as it crashed down and scraped along the shore with loud metallic graunching sounds and there was a general movement of both vehicles and foot passengers off and on?

My morning briefing to the passengers was to walk off the ferry, up the ramp at Kyleakin and climb aboard a blue bus which would be waiting for us.

I counted 18 on to the ferry --- 16 got off. It being fairly obvious that the two would realise their mistake I despatched the remainder of the party to Portree in the care of my regular coach driver who could manage perfectly well without me. The ferry returned – still no missing two so I returned to Lochalsh on it, just in time to see my two ladies dismounting from an InterCity bus – yes, it was blue – but about to depart for Glasgow.

"We looked round at the other people on the bus and didn't recognise anyone from our party – then my friend looked out of the window and said, "Mavis – this is where we got ON that ferry!""

Chapter 12

Most Passengers are Normal

Reading this treatise you could well be thinking that my Company's brochure attracted more than its fair share of oddballs. Untrue – I met and escorted hundreds of cheerful and well-adjusted people from all walks of life. Many contributed to the thick file of appreciative letters which I retain as a happy souvenir. It's the others one remembers!

And that memory is reinforced because the 'others' will often, but not always, be ostracised by the rest of the group and seek a disproportionate amount of the time and attention of the Tour Manager.

My usual introduction to a new party was commonly something like, "Good morning, folks. I'm Frank, your Tour Manager for the next few days," and then go into a briefing for the next timed activity.

Immediate interjection from a loud North Country voice, "My husband, Mr Green, and I do not believe in undue familiarity – we shall call you Mr Faulkner. Mr Green (she always referred to her husband thus) was a very important man in our community where he managed not one, but two large mills." This self-important pair was rapidly avoided by the rest and I had the dubious pleasure of their company for dinner every evening. Her loud, "Would you please be so kind as to pass (to rhyme with ass) the condiments to Mr Green?" raising barely-concealed titters around the dining room.

One very well-dressed lady appeared to go out of her way to be awkward and demanding – I feigned not to notice but I did ask my wife, who was travelling with me on this occasion, to see her to her seat on the train taking her home, whereupon she confessed, "I do find I get really good attention if I'm really bolshy". She had had the same attention as everyone else from me.

With parties of generally senior people there were few problems with timing with notable exceptions. Jean was always last – even if not late. A tiny lady with virtually no luggage other than a small carrier, she was usually greeted by a cheerful chorus of, "Come on, Jean," when she appeared. By a strange co-incidence she was on one of the first tours I did and, 20 years later, on almost one of the last. Her attitude, character, and carrier had not changed.

Escorting what were essentially Short Breaks I was quite often amazed by the amount of luggage, in vast suitcases, which some managed to drag behind them. There still appeared to be a wish to change into 'something different' for every dinner (usually the ladies I would add) but conversely I have clear memories of one elderly lady who always managed to be immaculate and colour co-ordinated out of one very small bag.

Many tours ended in Inverness from where we left on an early morning train necessitating a very early breakfast. It was prudent to have a headcount as breakfast progressed. Two were not there one morning but a telephone call to their room produced only an engaged tone from which I assumed they were up and about. Neighbours in the next room had seen their door open in confirmation of my assumption. Wrong!

Departure time was getting perilously close when I called at their room. Entering the open door I found them both asleep (but not for long) in bed. They had 15 minutes to get up, wash (optional), pack, dress and get to the nearby station. They made it – just.

"We left the door open because it had a funny lock and we were afraid we might get locked in (which took my mind straight back to my first tour). And we took the phone off the hook in case it rang in the night and disturbed us." Some people!

A similar incident very shortly after had a slightly different twist. The lady in question answered my phone call from the dining room – and promptly went back to sleep. I roused her only 10 minutes to the departure of the only London train of the day on which we were booked. She leapt into the bathroom with her clothes, dressed rapidly whilst I emptied the bedroom drawers into her suitcase. We both just made it!

I never had any problems from sleeping in different beds night after night and was usually up and about and taking a walk before breakfast to clear my mind for the day. Only once did I sleep in. We were due to leave our hotel in Orkney to catch a ferry at 9am. I woke and looked at my clock, confirmed what I thought it said from my watch, "Help!" and leapt out of bed at 8.30 – packed and nonchalantly joined the waiting passengers on the coach, confessing only to an "early breakfast!"

Inverness seems to have more memories than most – probably because many of the tours started or ended there. Preparing to leave the hotel at an even earlier time on a different tour all the party was present at the breakfast table but there was absolutely no sign of the kitchen staff to serve our early Continental breakfast. Grabbing a couple of 'volunteers' we rapidly produced some toast and coffee in the kitchen to the cheers of the remainder of the party. I left a steaming note for the hotel chef, a good friend, who on my next visit was profusely apologetic, whilst gently pointing out that what I had done was probably highly illegal. I don't admit to many illegalities but one sometimes had to take decisive action to keep the show on the road.

As a last resort against disruptive passengers most Tour Managers will carry a "Red Card" which can be used to terminate the holiday of a passenger whose behaviour is likely to be to the detriment of the running of their tour or affecting other passengers. (Read the small print, under "Conduct Whilst Travelling", next time you book a tour). To my knowledge the Red Card was only used once by the Company's representatives and that was in respect of a passenger with suicidal tendencies who kept threatening to jump off ferries.

Chapter 13

One of Our Hotels is Missing

The first day coffee-and-comfort stop on a Western Isles Tour out of Inverness was at the Station Hotel at Achnasheen where for several years we were greeted with tasty and generous refreshment at a very reasonable cost. Bidding them farewell on one occasion I checked in their diary that we were expected and booked in for two weeks later.

Arrival – two weeks later – I couldn't believe my eyes and seriously wondered if by some mischance we had arrived at the wrong place – of the Station Hotel there was simply No Trace. A closer search revealed the obvious footprint where it had been that was the sole evidence of a disastrous fire and complete site clearance since my previous visit.

Apart from my first tour I usually had foreknowledge if any hotel had been changed from that advertised, the excuse usually being 'computer error'. So it was with some surprise, coupled with amusement that, on our arrival at our booked hotel at Campbeltown at the tip of the Kintyre Peninsula, we were bumped to a nearby establishment because, "We're still full of International Observers who are here for the secret submarine trials!"

Not actually missing, but sorely missed, was the Lochboisdale Hotel where on many occasions we feasted on a sumptuous dinner whilst waiting for the evening ferry to Barra, which docked about 50 yards away. Mine host and his wife had arrived many years before and just never left, until age and retirement intervened. After a welcome dram in a friendly bar with a glowing peat fire the hotel always a produced generous home-made soup with fresh warm bread followed by such a superb succulent roast beef that many years later still has me salivating as I remember. And have you ever eaten such a meal when mine host circulates with unlimited seconds of meat?

Whilst the hotel is now alive again it stood for many years as an empty shell but always a reminder of many happy evenings waiting for the ferry.

Chapter 14

Favourite Places and Lost Cases

As an enthusiastic young map reader I was always fascinated by the chain of close but apparently unconnected islands stretching from Berneray to Barra through the Uists, Benbecula and Eriskay in the Western Isles so I grabbed the opportunity to visit them myself in 1992, after another tour ending in Inverness. By this time the islands were connected by causeways but were still a long journey from England by road and ferry. Although the journey from London could be accomplished by air in little more than two hours the cost, like other short journeys in small aircraft, is disproportionately high.

I had read that every boat has a Barra man in its crew so, when looking for somewhere to stay there, I found the Barra man on the ferry on which I was travelling to Shetland who simply said, "Ring my Mum when you get there!" Mum was unfortunately full that weekend. She passed me on to a friend, and I have now been staying on holidays there with Morag for 20 years. Further south in the chain of the Western Isles lies the small pretty island of Mingulay to which, when sea conditions are favourable, there are excursions by small boat from Barra. The boatman will normally need a minimum number of fare-paying passengers for this excursion to run. On two different opportunities when my wife was travelling with me the conditions for sailing were good but there was only one potential passenger, each of whom was prepared to charter the whole boat and invited my wife along. One man was the nephew of the last private owner of Mingulay and wished to visit for nostalgic reasons, the other an American folk singer desperate to see the island from where Mingulay Boat Song came. On both these occasions I was unable to travel with her and it was another 10 years before my chance came.

Seeing the potential for the sort of like-minded people whose company I had enjoyed over the previous few years I encouraged the Boss to operate tours to the Western Isles – which ran successfully for many years – with me accompanying most of course! A host of travel books and now websites will extol the pristine beauty of these wonderful islands to which I need not add but, as usual, the overwhelming memories of that beauty will forever be a backdrop to a few tours unforgettable for other reasons.

Like 'The Tale of Two Ladies.'

Settling down in my room on Benbecula at the end of a long, unusually hot and tiring day I was summoned to reception where two of the ladies in my party had already arrived. No 1 was totally hysterical and almost incapable of speech. She had somehow managed to lock herself into her room from which she had been unable to escape. Passers-by were attracted to her plight by her screaming cries of "HELP" as she hung half out of a sloping roof velux window. Having been released with a master key her main complaint, between sobs, was that she would be trapped in her room in case of fire. We could never make out how she managed her self-incarceration but moved her to another room anyway.

Then lady No 2, who stood patiently watching this pantomime, quietly said, "I've left my case in my hotel room in Inverness". Ok, action, lateral thinking – first thing – round up my coach driver to visit the local Co-op store before it closed to purchase necessary overnight supplies which were apparently toothbrush and toothpaste, clean knickers and tights and a half bottle of Scottish medicine.

But how to recover a case from a hotel which, by this time, was now 8 hours, 2 ferries and 3 islands away? (A quick look at map will highlight the problem). Having been on this circuit for some years I now had a good and trusted network of people in the right places through which I initiated a recovery plan of which I'm still proud.

At the Inverness hotel the head porter agreed to collect the bag and hand it to the driver of the service bus heading for Oban the next day. At Oban a porter from a hotel near the bus stop also agreed to take possession of the case and hand it to the purser of the Barra-bound ferry from whom we would collect it when travelling on that boat from Lochboisdale that evening. It all worked according to plan – one impressed passenger – one relieved TM.

It was at the same Benbecula hotel some years later that we arrived from Kyle of Lochalsh with too many suitcases – the extras had labels with a Brussels address and there had been a Belgian coach party staying at the same hotel the previous night.

Neither the driver nor I could possibly imagine how this could have occurred. I warned the Lochalsh hotel which we had left that there would be a shout for missing cases at some time – and that I held them in the Western Isles.

Later that day I got a call from the Tour Manager of the Belgian party which had just been dispatched on a ferry heading for the Continent. Before I could say anything he told me that it was no – one's fault other than the owner of the cases who – contrary to instructions – had personally loaded the cases into the boot of our coach quite oblivious of the fact that whilst their vehicle was vast and yellow, ours was small and red.

Two suitcases stolen from a train in Scotland, off a luggage rack immediately behind the loser from my party, were never recovered, whilst a suitcase which disappeared from a coach luggage locker in Scotland resurfaced many months later at Victoria Coach Station in London with the contents intact.

The most brazen theft of suitcases was at a hotel reception when two cases were removed from beside the legs of a customer who was checking in at a high counter.

Chapter 15

Double Trouble

The next scenario is on a day trip by rail from Aylesbury to Weymouth with various tour options both en route and at the destination. Those tours normally attracted two distinct types of passenger: those just going for a day out by train to the seaside, and a few rail freaks who would be able to travel some track or manoeuvre not normally performed by a regular timetabled train or in the type of train being used on that day.

So it was somewhat of a surprise to find two elderly gents aboard with a carrier bag full of cans of beer which they quietly got stuck into as we went along.

To ensure that all went smoothly there was a company representative in each carriage and a general announcement invited the passengers to contact us with any problem or special request.

"Excuse me, mate," from one of the imbibers, "Could we stop at Southampton?" (not being a scheduled stop). "Why?" I asked. "There's a good British Legion club there!" Request denied as some of the more rail-extreme passengers had come specifically to travel non-stop through Southampton (whatever turns you on!).

They accepted my explanation with good grace but whooped with delight on arrival at Weymouth where they found a British Legion club right opposite the railway station.

A good time seems to have been enjoyed by all – including this pair who were noted returning to the train direct from the club, each carrying a six-pack. As the journey homewards continued they continued supping gently and quietly and, inevitably, fell asleep sprawled across the table in front of them.

When the train stopped with a jerk at Reading, late on a Saturday night, they woke with a start and made for the exit. Only one made it – the doors closed and locked leaving the other standing and bemused, but at Slough he managed to exit safely and was last seen wandering along the platform.

A short time later the Boss came through the train and noted their disappearance. "Funny thing," I said. "One got off at Reading, the other at Slough." "Even funnier," said the Boss. "They both got on at Aylesbury!"

Chapter 16

But Some Folks are Difficult to Understand

It was not a Company policy to sell the front seats on coach touring journeys. By sometimes sitting towards the rear of a coach instead of at the front in the courier seat I was well aware that visibility other than to the side was very limited in the high-backed seats of a modern coach, especially for smaller people. On my first briefing I always suggested moving seats from day to day. This gave everyone a chance to move around although not everyone would be able to occupy a front seat during short breaks of 4-6 days, and those who made a beeline for the front seats on the first journey were usually quite happy to share this benefit subsequently. But it was quite remarkable how most people habitually returned to the seat they first occupied.

The only exception, I explained, was for the benefit of lesser-able people who sometimes requested a particular seat. So it was not surprising when a pair of elderly ladies asked if they could occupy the front seats for the whole of the tour, 'as we are not very good coach travellers'. One had to wonder why they had booked a coach tour. I granted this facility and explained to the rest of the party the reason, which would have been more generously received if this pair had not rapidly gone to sleep within minutes of starting most journeys.

Other than that, and despite their significant ages, they were able to take a full part in the tour and the activities offered over 5 days. Approaching Kings Cross on the last day of the tour I knew that they would have to cross London to their next train and asked if they needed any advice or help when we reached the station.

"No thank you – we cross by ambulance!"

As the train slowed they both donned previously-unseen surgical collars, produced and extended telescopic walking sticks and waited patiently on board until their pre-booked assistance arrived.

Quite the opposite was a very small couple I discovered hidden on the back seat of a coach two days into a tour. Although I had counted my party on and off the vehicle several times already, I really didn't remember seeing this pair before. They were on my tour but I couldn't help noticing afterwards that they were so quiet and totally undemanding as to be almost invisible.

There were several occasions when on arrival at Mull or Orkney off a ferry the crowds from the boat split into different tour parties to leave from a line of coaches parked at the quayside. I don't remember losing anyone on those occasions but often had to evict a few passengers from less well-briefed parties when my headcount was excessive.

Many people from the island of Mull commute daily on the regular CalMac ferry to Oban and it was a point of amusement amongst the regular commuters that one individual almost invariably only scraped aboard the last ferry of the day with seconds to spare. On the day before one of my crossings I was regaled with his latest adventure. He is running towards the ferry which is about two feet away from the pier – takes a flying leap and is hauled aboard by the brawny arms of two seamen. Loud applause from the watching audience – the ferry was coming IN!

Chapter 17

Fogbound

Ferries usually continue to sail in fog. Planes are less likely to fly, so it was often touch and go for our helicopter flights to and from the Isles of Scilly.

On this occasion thick fog persisted over the isles throughout the morning and early afternoon so our chances of the helicopter or fixed-wing aircraft coming to lift us off the island were diminishing. The weather forecast promised no improvement. The usual itinerary planned a morning flight to Penzance, giving a choice of afternoon trains onwards.

Delays cause little concern for island hotels – if passengers could not leave there would be few balancing inward customers and so their accommodation was not empty but still earning money. After that problems arose some days on the normally well-filled helicopter flights, with passenger numbers building up, following a service disruption, for the few vacant seats available.

The choice which I had to accept in lieu of any alternative was to transfer the party to the island passenger vessel the 'Scillonian' which would sail through the fog even if arrival in Penzance would be too late to catch any day train onwards. At this late stage I was unable to reserve any berths on the sleeper train from Penzance other than in person at the Penzance ticket office. As we sailed slowly eastwards the inevitable "Law of Sodde" took over: the fog cleared, and from the slow-moving ferry we were able to see helicopter flights scurrying back and forth to St Mary's.

Penzance was overfull with other displaced passengers so I was not surprised to find the night sleeper train to London reported fully booked by the ticket office – likewise most of the hotels where I had tried to find some beds for my passengers. I eventually found rooms for some in Penzance, the balance in Mousehole and booked shuttle transport with our local reliable coach operator to get them there, and back to the station the following morning.

Six passengers were, however, quite adamant that they MUST be in London by the following day.

I ran the sleeper train manager to ground in Penzance station and confessed to my dilemma. He confirmed that the train was indeed full but after a recount encouraged by a couple of Bank of England tokens, three second class double berths were found and available if my first class passengers, normally entitled to single berths, would agree to share. They really didn't have any options.

Not being pre-booked on the sleeper we had to pay for our berths and I expected that we would be covered by the delay clause in our travel insurance. The people I left in Cornwall enjoyed an extra day's holiday, all fully re-imbursed by their travel insurance, but those who had incurred extra cost to get home on the sleeper had their claims rejected as they "had not been delayed by more than 24 hours" (but one of the Boss's persuasive letters in his inimitable style achieved an ex-gratia payment for them).

A claim for the difference between first and second class fare by one who was already travelling free on a rail company first class pass was given short shrift in another of the Boss's missiles.

I can recall only one occasion when a normally-reliable CalMac ferry was delayed by more than a few hours by adverse weather. A colleague, stranded on the Isle of Harris with a hen party of senior civil servants, managed to keep them entertained with an invite to a ceilidh where, by custom, the bottle circulated freely. Most needed confirmation the following morning that "Yes" they had really enjoyed themselves.

Chapter 18

Parties of a Certain Age

From my time with Age Concern I knew that ladies under about 70 are very coy about their age – but after 80 proudly declare, "You wouldn't think I was – n years!" The blokes, by and large, just got on with life and I was generally unaware of their ages – in fact it was often difficult to tell the difference between the young 80's and the old 60's. A notable exception was a retired East Coast Top Link steam loco driver – these were the supermen who drove the non-stop trains from Kings Cross to Edinburgh and he, like many others I met, had been quite happy to lend a hand with the shovel – that's apparently how the firemen learned to drive! I think the info came from an ex-colleague on the same tour that he was 92 years old – probably my oldest-ever passenger.

I rapidly discovered that most, "I've forgotten my tablets", were solved by another in the same party on the same medication until we reached the next pharmacist. Although these tended to be few and far between in the places to which we went in Orkney, Shetland and the Western Isles, local pharmacists were cheerfully prepared to dispense out-of-hours.

This proved to be the case on an afternoon on Hoy – a reasonably remote Northern island – particularly on a Sunday afternoon. I had noticed that one of my elderly ladies seemed to be in considerable discomfort. She eventually admitted to suffering with cystitis. She couldn't imagine finding a doctor there or even on Mainland Orkney on a Sunday afternoon but was mightily relieved, and totally amazed, when I introduced her to the island GP – who just happened to be a crew member of the Longhope lifeboat which we were visiting at the time. He confirmed her self-diagnosis and arranged that the chemist in Stromness would dispense the pills she needed on our return – on Sunday evening.

Sea sickness rarely bothered my people but I vividly remember a particularly rough crossing from Shetland when even I wasn't feeling too perky and found relief in being horizontal on my bunk – from which I was thrown out at one particular rough moment. Sometime during the night I was summoned to a cabin where one of my elderlies was in a very poor way. If you haven't encountered it I can confirm that near-unconscious elderly ladies who have been copiously sick over themselves in the confines of a small cabin on a boat as stable as a crazy rocking horse is not the world's most pleasant sight – and I wasn't feeling too well either!

I summoned the purser and together we fed her tablets until they stopped coming back and she seemed to settle into a deep sleep (or was it a coma?) In those far-off days ships' pursers carried vast quantities of a particular make of anti-motion sickness pills – the only ones, to my knowledge, which rarely failed to work. They handed these out generously – not least to reduce the amount of cleaning up the vessel after a rough voyage – but I suspect that this practice has now ceased,

I spent the rest of that night worrying about my passenger and felt pretty ragged in the morning – after very little sleep and continuing rough conditions. She, on the other hand, appeared bright and chirpy with no memory of the night's activities although obviously aware of her state on awakening. "What did you give me? That's the best night's sleep I've had in years."

Conversely, one pair were quite determined to be seasick on a very short crossing and despite my forecast that we were going to have a near-perfect crossing on a glassy sea to Orkney took their tablets at the correct interval before boarding. It was a perfect crossing – they were sick.

One of my elderly passengers who was rather unsteady on his feet suffered a total collapse at dinner on the first evening of his tour. Paramedics appeared within seconds from the next-door hospital – where I visited him the following day. By that time he was recovering although clearly quite unwell but the reason for his unsteady gait, a false leg, greeted me from the foot of his bed. He was not due to be discharged for some days so I had to say farewell in Fort William and continue that particular tour. Not unnaturally his wife chose to stay near him and I made arrangements for her to be accommodated at the hotel and subsequently travel homewards on the sleeper from Fort William.

Having incurred considerable extra expense we helped submit a claim on his travel insurance policy. The company rejected the claim on behalf of his wife: "there being no reason why Mrs X could not have continued her holiday." After considerable representation by our ace letter writer they reluctantly agreed to settle the claim in full, but as an ex-gratia sum without an admission of liability.

And this story had a rather pleasing sequel. The gentleman was clearly quite unwell when I last visited him in hospital and I really feared for his future. However, 12 months later I received a phone call from him asking if I would join him for dinner at the same hotel in Fort William – he and his wife were just starting the same tour where it had been so dramatically interrupted previously. By extreme good fortune and an amazing co-incidence I was to be in the town on the date he mentioned and we celebrated together.

Chapter 19

Of Baths and Bathing

In the '80s customers often asked specifically for a bath, not a shower, with their accommodation and were not unduly daunted if it wasn't en suite but there has been a noticeable change of attitude towards personal ablutions in the last 25 years.

Latterly, requests for a bath, not a shower, were rare indeed and an expectation of en suite is taken for granted.

In those far-off days before EC, when Water Interference seemed not to have permeated to the Far North or the Western Isles this sometimes meant that the taps of some establishments in these areas dispensed the most delicious soft water – albeit sometimes tea-like brown – with bits.

Occasional cries of, "I couldn't have a bath, the water was all dirty!" were usually outnumbered by ladies being late for dinner. These were the ones who, accustomed to living in hard-water areas, had spent ages trying to rinse their normal amount of shampoo out of their hair. Alas, the long tentacles of the EC have reached the remotest areas who now share awful-tasting, heavily-chlorinated water with the rest of us after huge investment in purifying plant.

Two taps on a bath are easily understood, but anyone used to staying in hotels will know that there are as many varieties of shower and permutations of control as there are hotels. Demonstrations were sometimes needed – forewarned at premises where I knew that their controls seemed to have been designed for people with a three-digit IQ. I have yet to encounter a brand of shower which has more than 1 mm of adjustment between freezing cold and scalding hot; except on board ferries where scalding hot is the norm – with appropriate Health and Safety warnings, of course.

In the sin bin to the rest of a party was an elderly gent whose personal hygiene, evidenced by an aura of stale body odours, left much to be desired. I gently enquired if all aspects of his accommodation were satisfactory. All were, including both the bath and the shower, "but I won't need to use them. I had a bath last week!" (which I didn't really believe!).

As a complete alternative to all the above I took a special friend with my party to the Edinburgh Tattoo and our stay at a vast hotel in the centre of Glasgow co-incided with a complete lack of water – hot or cold – thanks to an unrelated utility severing a water main in the adjacent street.

The Edinburgh Tattoo has never cancelled one of its open-air performances on the exposed parade ground of Edinburgh Castle. If inclement weather looked likely I usually issued our passengers with two bin-liners. Sitting in one and pulling the other over the shoulders kept us reasonably dry – but not warm.

Chapter 20

Ireland – Somewhere Else

Picture a small railway station with two tracks and two platforms. One platform is almost completely full of people. The opposite one is quite empty until a solitary figure appears on it; he shouts across, "Does anybody know which platform the next train goes from?" Only in Ireland!

I was not destined to visit the southern part of Ireland until later in my Tour Managing hobby. Irish railways were largely constructed for passengers, Guinness and peat but by 2003, although still widely-used, were threatened by complete closure. On my first visit all the railstaff were on strike – well, an Irish strike. All were on duty, trains were running normally, our reserved seats were identified, but passengers were not being charged fares. What a pity that we had pre-booked tickets.

Fast-forward a few years: enter the Celtic Tiger with limitless money seemingly available and you find an almost complete new railway, new tracks, new stations, new signalling and new trains, even to the extreme of flying in new 100-ton locomotives from Canada, in the giant Russian Antanov freighter.

Trains were widely used in the south where the roads left much to be desired and there was limited car ownership – although the Tiger sorted that to some extent, Irish trains are still well-used and quite a different travelling experience. My Company's briefing notes warned (advised?) our passengers that on Irish trains the locals will not just speak to you, but engage in lengthy conversations and, not infrequently, sing! I was to encounter all these aspects on several subsequent journeys.

Ticket collectors, noting the English-issued tickets, would ask where were you from (*ah, I have a cousin there*) where were you going to (*a lovely place*) and were you enjoying your holiday? (*of course you will*).

The modern Irish trains are very comfortable and smooth-running as they glide along on a largely rebuilt railway where the tracks are 5'3" apart – the Irish gauge – also found in Victoria, Australia where the first railway had an Irish Engineer. But there can still be Interesting Problems.

We were awaiting our early morning train, the first out from Rosslare Town, when a railwayman appeared from a signal box further along the line and ran towards us to explain that our train was delayed due to a communication failure. He ran back to his box, pulled a few levers, dropped some signals and allowed a train into our platform – but not our train. The 'communication failure?' Our train had been parked BEHIND the second train due out – on a 'single-track' siding!

Later that same day we arrived at Limerick Junction where the main platform is used bi-directionally and trains exit from it both east and west. The station announcer repeatedly and clearly told us that the first train from this platform was for Dublin, the second, for which we were waiting, was for Killarney. "Important information for passengers on Platform 1 – the Dublin train has been delayed by cows on the line – therefore the first train will be for Killarney and the second train will be for Dublin." This was repeated several times before we boarded our train for Killarney – together with a good number of people who thought they were going to Dublin! But there were no alarms when this became known and it was not long before the Dublin-bound, who seemed to have enjoyed a successful day at the races somewhere but were now heading west, were well into the second verse of "Danny Boy" having checked out all the English passengers.

And where would a query to the driver of a train to ascertain the exact time of departure be answered by, "I tink I go when da man waves his little flag an' blows his little whistle." Or where you would be greeted by your coach driver,

"We're going to have a good day today – I've just come straight from Mass." He later entertained us along the way with Irish songs and the multiple verses of 'The Wild Colonial Boy' prompted by our entry into Castlemaine whence the boy came.

Unfortunately, on that tour, whilst the hotel had been completely refurbished at a cost of tens of millions of Euros (the Tiger was still roaring) the food was atrocious. I clearly remember the 'Chef's selection of fresh local vegetables' – lumpy part-cooked potatoes, ditto carrots and swede. Quite justifiably many complaints were received both at the hotel and our Head Office. They were passed, as usual, to the hotel to rectify.

The complainants each received a fat glossy brochure highlighting the millions of Euros spent on the refurbishing, with several complimentary copies for the Company.

Chapter 21

Try This at Euston

We're just finishing breakfast at my favourite hotel in Inverness and there's plenty of time for us all to pack and catch the train from the adjacent station in just over an hour's time heading towards the Western Isles.

"Got a little problem, Frank!" says elderly gent. "I had a little op a couple of weeks ago and today is the last day that I can have my stitches out."

No, don't say, "Why didn't you think of that before now?" – action needed, and fast.

Brief hotel receptionist to call local major hospital and also book a taxi – elderly gent to pack and take suitcase with him – knowing my current run of luck he could be admitted. Brief him what to do and how to contact the Office if he is.

Run to station crew room and ascertain that friend Hector, as usual, will be driving the train we should be catching – he owes me a favour.

"I've got an emergency, Hector – can you hang on a bit – shouldn't be too long?"

"OK, Frank, but don't push yer luck."

Taxi arrives and departs with stitch in situ – returns one hour later with large plaster on top of scalp in lieu. The train has waited for us beyond its scheduled departure time.

Postcard to the Boss: "Try this at Euston!"

It was at the same station following a surfeit of Scottish weather that we boarded a train which was virtually all-over brown where windblown soil had adhered to wet train. View through windows approximately nil and we were about to traverse what has been described by more than one traveller as the country's most spectacular rail journey.

I sought the station foreman (now an extinct breed) and complained that we had come specially for this journey but would see virtually nothing.

Without thinking he said, "Just make sure that all the windows are shut (it was possible to open them then) if you don't mind being a few minutes late."

Exit Inverness station via the carriage washer.

Another postcard to the Boss

Approaching Queen Street station in Glasgow on what should have been a limited-stop train it became clear that we were trapped behind a local stopping service. It was imperative that some of my party caught a specific connection at Glasgow, failing which they would not have been able to reach Cornwall that day. After consultation with the conductor and the driver, Control agreed to side-line the previous train and send us fast and first into Queen Street with green signals all the way to a simple cross-platform change to a delayed service. This Glasgow-Edinburgh express shuttle was ScotRail's prestige service and could not be delayed without incurring the wrath of the ScotRail MD. However, on this occasion it had suffered a 'slight technical door problem' which was resolved as soon as my passengers jumped aboard.

The Boss is getting used to my postcards.

On another occasion this same service was running very late leaving little enough time to get across Glasgow to Central station and we were in our booked seats at the rear end of the train. At my suggestion to save precious minutes on arrival we all managed, with suitcases, to push through the length of a very full train to the front coach.

At the top of the steep descent into Queen Street is a triangle of railway lines along which our train normally took the right hand option. On this day it took the left-hand line and then REVERSED down the third arm into the station, a manoeuvre I had never encountered before on a train in service. We were back at the rear of the train again.

Things seemed to happen to me on the West Highland line. Some months after being interviewed on the train by a reporter from Radio Scotland I was called forward to compare notes with the driver, who had also been involved in that programme. We rounded a slight bend at a slowish speed to find a tractor and trailer parked across the track. There was plenty of time to stop the train and the driver castigated the farmer who merely explained that he hadn't realised it was the first day of the summer timetable and that the train times had altered.

Chapter 22

In Which the Tour Manager Gets Left Behind

I am only aware of one instance where the party left without the Tour Manager who was refused onward transportation, although I had despatched parties a couple of times in the care of a trusted coach driver and caught them up later.

It was a near-run thing with yours truly many years ago, on a day trip to Paris. It was usual in those days to collect all the passports and hand them en bloc to the French Immigration officer on the Eurostar train heading for Paris. The only problem on this occasion was that I had forgotten mine. They always seemed to be returned far too quickly for any check to have been made. I kept quiet. They didn't notice. One illegal immigrant.

I know for certain on another occasion that the Immigration Officer had examined my passport. He handed it back to me with a smile and a "Happy Birthday, Mr Faulkner."

One group in the care of a colleague was due to fly from Birmingham to the Isle of Man when photo identity for internal flights wasn't being universally sought. All the group, however, had suitable photo identity except the Tour Manager and he was denied boarding. He had no option but to wave his group goodbye and rush home, some 60 miles away, to collect his passport – but that was only half the solution. By this time there wasn't another flight to the island from Birmingham – but there was an evening flight from Liverpool. He travelled to Liverpool and successfully joined a flight – for which his photo identity was NOT wanted.

Which reminds me of the first tour to Alderney which I set up and managed. I had visited Alderney in 1975, on shore leave from a cruise on TS Winston Churchill which I was evaluating for its possible value to the Police Cadets I was training. I was so impressed by my very brief stay that I determined to return but it was another 30 years before I did so in 2005. I was bowled over by the beauty and tranquillity of Alderney.

In those early days the Boss was prepared to let a tour run at only a marginal profit. One or two ran at a loss but our faithful regular customers appreciated that, when they found themselves in a small party, there wasn't a lot of benefit to the Company and we gained much goodwill and return bookings. (Also much nicer for the TM!).

It was uncannily possible to predict which tours would not attract sufficient custom almost as soon as bookings opened.

If a tour was to be cancelled for lack of numbers it was normal to give any booked passengers at least six weeks' notice. At this time it was also possible to extricate the Company from provisional hotel bookings without undue penalty.

The first Alderney tour had only booked a dozen (almost a Trislander plane-full) but marginally profitable. Then, suddenly, days before the tour, six cancellations came through – all for medical emergencies, so there was no great loss for those people: they were covered by our travel insurance. This was made compulsory for all after a traumatic incident involving open heart surgery in a foreign country – and yes, he was covered for the six-figure sum for hospital attention and air ambulance evacuation.

I met the party at Brighton International (formerly Shoreham), a beautiful Art Deco airport and found them all to be quite elderly. Our customer database was getting older and the tour had attracted some of our faithful following who had been everywhere else in our brochure – sometimes more than once.

We were left with six for Alderney. It was too late to cancel our contractual agreement with the hotel or the airline so the Boss just shrugged and let the tour run. Mindful of its new status Brighton International demanded photo identification – but only two had any. The other four did not hold either a passport or a photo driving licence. Am I going to have a party of two? After a long conversation the local Immigration Officer came over to view the party and accepted that four eighty-year-olds did not represent a terrorist threat – but he examined their walking sticks meticulously first.

Our return flight from Alderney hit the same problem but the airport accepted that as I must have been able to establish convincing reasons for Brighton to allow the outward flight they didn't really want to incarcerate four elderly people on the island indefinitely.

When another small party appeared to be a likelihood the Boss suggested that if I would drive a minibus it would be possible to remove the cost of a 50-seater coach and still run the tour. And so it was. My wife came along on this occasion. Observing the help needed to load and unload our passengers some other guests at the hotel enquired, "Are they from a care home?" This did not seem to be the sort of publicity which the Company would seek so I played it down significantly and made sure that no material with our name on was visible.

Chapter 23

What Else Can You Lose?

With quite a few one-night stays in hotels it was inevitable that some items got lost or forgotten. Most small bathroom items are replaceable along the way but – what about bus seats?

For a slightly larger-than-usual party the Command Bunker confirmed that the three coach suppliers had vehicles with enough seats although one had only just enough – the same number of seats as passengers. Coaches 1 and 2 were used without problem but when coach 3 was loaded the vehicle was one seat short – impossible – 54 passengers, including the TM, and the writing on the coach clearly stated, "To seat 54 passengers." OK, all seats are occupied, no strangers on board, so let's count the seats – there were actually 53! And the coach had been in use for a year or two but clearly never contained the same number of passengers as the number painted on the side.

Passengers occasionally went missing, although rarely for more than an hour or two. A new TM on his first assignment dropped his passengers at Pooley Bridge in the Lake District with a return time sufficient to allow the vehicle to meet our return charter train at Oxenholme. Come the appointed time he was one single man missing and waited as long as he dare but eventually left without him, arriving at the station with literally minutes to spare. We never heard from the missing man – why? If he just wanted a single journey he could have told us. Nowt so queer as folk!

A variation on the missing seat or passenger is the missing driver. Annually released from his depot duties to drive for a tour to the Outer Hebrides – with the excuse of testing a new or refurbished vehicle, Hamish [I dare not use his real name, even after many years] always requested this perk and his driving could not be faulted, other than being driven to distraction by the merest squeak or rattle in a new vehicle.

Soon after our arrival in Stornoway he always disappeared in quick time – returning like the prodigal some hours later – very happy but almost unable to stand. He had managed to return to base from a very short session on one occasion and commenced circulating around the party at dinner, uttering the most foul oaths (for want of a better adjective) and clearly, as usual, almost unable to stand. He was apparently allergic to the Trawler Rum which his friends on the island insisted was good for him. I quickly became aware of the situation and ushered and part-carried him up the stairs to his bedroom. I scuppered an intention to visit a local disco that evening by removing most of his clothes and shoes and locking him in his room. He was snoring gently in a heap behind the door when I returned some time later. I left him there with visions of looking for another driver the next day. By the next morning he was sleeping peacefully across his bed and after a few cups of coffee seemed none the worse for his experience.

Later in the day I was buttonholed by one of our lovely elderly lady passengers to whom he had been particularly coarse and offensive. Expecting a fully justified complaint I was completely bowled over by her comment, "Wasn't Hamish funny last night, pretending to be drunk!"

Occasionally drivers (and coaches) unaccountably went missing or failed to meet us at a pre-arranged booked rendezvous. It fortunately never happened to me when the programme could not be rapidly re-scheduled and the coach company's cage rattled. On one such occasion when the party was due to be conveyed along narrow Highland roads in two smaller coaches the owner and driver of the first told me that he was a driver missing, "Could I drive a bus?" Reply, "Yes," and I did. John later asked how long I had held a PSV licence and I replied, "Never." "But you told me you had." "You asked me if I could drive a bus, John – my answer was correct." With hindsight this was possibly not one of my wisest decisions but fortunately all passed off without problems and I kept the show on the road.

It was the same John, sadly now in the big bus garage in the sky, whose bus died half-way round Loch Ness. The mechanic who was called out took one sniff of the fuel tank and I can still recall his soft Highland voice, "You got petrol in here, John – that's why it's no going." John was quite adamant that he had filled the vehicle himself and no way would he put petrol into his much-loved diesel bus – but petrol it was and some time elapsed before the Original Nessie Bus took to the roads again.

Chapter 24

Our Train Gets the Red Card

Day trips to Blackpool were quite notorious for losing passengers – on this occasion we lost our train.

Before the days of automatic train door locking it was normal that platform staff checked visually, and in cases of doubt physically, that all carriage doors were shut. If all the large brass door handles could be seen to be in a horizontal position they were safe on departure from the station. It was not totally unknown whilst the train was in motion for passengers to try the door handles, sometimes with catastrophic effect, but more usually just leaving the outside door handles askew indicating possible insecurity.

The coaches on our Blackpool train were of a type with a central access door in addition to the door at either end of the carriage. To avoid any possible problems of access at the stations, where we paused but not to pick up passengers, these central doors were locked out of use and secure but at some the handles were tried, albeit unsuccessfully. As a result some handles were NOT horizontal.

Misaligned door handles could be, and often were, picked up by signalmen. This would result in the train being stopped at the next signal and all the door locks checked. Inevitably this led to delays, both to the stopped train, and increasingly to following services.

The signalmen in the North-West seem to have been a particularly sharp-eyed breed and our train was stopped three times for door handle checks before reaching Blackpool resulting in serious delays to many services in that area.

On arrival at Blackpool we were met by a real jobsworth, florid of face and extreme of speech, waving the equivalent of a Red Card. No amount of explanation was accepted or even listened to and our train was shunted off into a siding until an engineer could attend and declare it to be safe – and that would be 2 days later, on the following Monday.

And we had a train load of passengers to return south that evening.

I will never know how he managed it but after many hours of negotiation the Boss worked one of his major miracles and we all returned home in a much nicer and more modern train.

But the following morning someone would be making a frantic search for the InterCity Blackpool to Brighton train which, by then, would be parked somewhere in West London.

Chapter 25

Now There's A Funny Thing

When open staff appraisal reporting was introduced in my Police Force I discovered that I had been criticised for an 'Inability to Delegate'. On appeal I got this re-worded as 'Leads from the Front' which is just what every Tour Manager does all the time.

On the tour circuit I encountered incidents which appealed to what my staff appraisal reports had also referred to, and called 'a strange sense of humour, not always understood or appreciated.'

Looking for an updated Blue Guide to Scotland in the excellent Shetland bookshop in Lerwick I was directed to the travel guide section where I was quite unable to find it.

"Did you no look in the FOREIGN section?" queried the assistant with great emphasis on the 'foreign'.

I met a couple of whom I had been warned, arriving amongst others at Aberdeen station. The man had repeatedly telephoned the office querying both the holiday and his booking conditions. His wife indicated that we should hang back when the party left the station and explained that her husband was rather hard of hearing and difficult to deal with. "Has she told you I'm deaf?" he bellowed as we caught up with him. He turned out to be excellent jovial company with a fund of amusing stories which only a Harley Street surgeon could tell.

A little old Cockney couple were the life and soul of the party. Wherever he was there was irrepressible laughter. "Is he like this at home," I queried, "and doesn't it become rather wearing after a time?" "Actually," she replied, "He has quietened down a lot since he gave up smoking."

This scene is a Sunday morning train from Inverness to Aberdeen. The four large louts who asked for four half-returns were quite clearly above the half-fare age but the conductor obliged without demur and sold them tickets at about £20 each. "It's a pity that one of you is not an adult," he said, answered by a joint aggressive grunt of "Why?" "Well, that one would have been £20 and the others £1 each. Next fare please." I later complimented him on his action which I thought worthy of commendation. "But please don't write to the firm," he pleaded. "You'd get me sacked!"

My coach driver and I were sitting on the wide windowsill of Barra Airport, Terminal 1, when a car appeared, fast, missing our toes by inches and crashed into the back of a parked car. "I've told you not to park your car there, John," she said. "I've crashed into it – AGAIN!"

"Sorry," the totally innocent driver replied.

That same coach driver had a well-appreciated sense of fun and on one trip we encountered an old mini-van, stationary on a single track road on Skye. Its driver was looking hard right, with no other thought than possibly counting his sheep on the hills and quite oblivious of any other traffic. Stuart cruised silently right up to the mini-van and parked the coach about 3 feet in front of it. It doesn't take a lot of imagination to visualise the reaction of the mini-van driver on looking forward. He took it in good part and had a good laugh with us.

There wasn't a room available for a single man who was desperate to book a Skye tour. The Boss asked if I would share a room. I reluctantly agreed. My 80-year old room-mate was perfectly companionable and mostly considerate but as a lifelong non-smoker I did draw the line at someone who wanted a puff of his foul pipe last thing at night and on waking!

On one other occasion I shared a cabin, on a well-booked cruise to Orkney and Shetland. I only found out afterwards that he was a vicar for whom it must have been a mind-broadening experience with a fund of material for his next few sermons.

I encountered quite a few passengers making nostalgic visits to Orkney and Shetland. Some had been stationed there during the war. Sometimes their parents had. A pair of elderly ladies spent a lot of their tour giggling/reminiscing about the time when they were amongst the small number of Wrens on the island of Hoy who had armed guards to protect them from the thousands of sailors also stationed there. But it did appear that they were sometimes able to escape their custodians.

It total contrast, one very brave lady had been steeling herself for many years to visit the remains of the site of the military airfield at Sullom Voe whence her husband flew off in his Catalina and was never heard of again.

Chapter 26

People R Interesting

The close proximity to others in a generally small tour party creates a greater possibility of interchange than meeting casual acquaintances briefly. It was always interesting to note the group dynamics and wonder which couples would end the tour as permanent friends at the end of five days.

It was never my practice to enquire what work my customers did, or might have done, probably anticipating their enquiry of me on the same subject. Everyone seems to have very strong opinions on the current shortcomings of the Police which can monopolise conversation. I was proud of what I did, but that was a long time ago when the job was easier, less subject to political interference and less controversial. So I often didn't tell.

Most guessers labelled me as an ex-schoolteacher. I had considered this after my indecently early retirement but in retrospect the fact that I didn't go that way seems to have been one of my more sensible decisions.

I was far more concerned that my parties acted as a harmonious group towards an enjoyable and rewarding short break. Details of employment could sometimes intrude. There was the occasional person or couple who tried to impress with past deeds and high-powered employment. They were often given short shrift. There was a tight bond between ex-railwaymen who seemed to recognise each other and often drifted into the nostalgia of past railway glories whilst deprecating the present. Personally I think that trains are now faster, cleaner and more regular than ever before – unfortunately they do suffer from a public perception of unacceptable delays incompatible with the highest rail fares in Europe at a time of exponential increase in passenger numbers.

Others who suspected a common interest within me often opened up on mutual interests and travels.

I encouraged parties to circulate meal by meal but the groups who coalesced at their first meal often tended to stick together for the rest of their tour. I always made sure, so far as possible, that I was the last person seated at dinner. Hotels without imagination or consideration could set tables for, say, fours for a party which did not divide by four. This could be embarrassing for one latecomer finding himself sitting alone, although on one occasion I knew that the party had plotted to ensure that this happened. If anyone had to sit alone or sweep up a singleton, it must be me.

An extremely upright and delightful old gentleman was dressed throughout in camel cords and a worn Harris Tweed jacket with leather elbow patches and cuffs. With a tightly-clipped military moustache and accent to match he was referred to by all as 'The General' though I knew, but didn't divulge, that he was just a Major (Rtd). He will be appearing again in this journal.

'Minnie Mouse' was the epithet accorded to one of my younger passengers whose big hair was always tied in a large bow which looked like ears from behind.

A charming and fit lady of 84 admitted to be considering retiring from a voluntary job delivering meals on wheels when she discovered that she was actually older than all her recipients.

In the midst of dinner one evening a man, whom the others had assumed was with his lady wife, but who I knew was not, startled them by looking at his watch then jumping up, saying, "I must ring my wife!"

The threesome of an elderly couple and a very smart dolly were assumed to be a couple and their daughter. It didn't seem to worry them when they regularly had to explain that they were a married couple – and her mother.

Conversations between groups frequently ranged around past worldwide holidays to just about every part of the globe from the Tropics to Antarctica. One had to admire an elderly widow who had paddled up the Amazon in a native canoe as an antidote to encroaching self-pity.

When an elderly lady passenger, who just happened to be an ex-teacher of my wife, expressed a wish to visit the grave of a particularly appreciated lecturer from her Uni days, that was accomplished. We found the site, and the grave slab, at Southend, at the tip of the Kintyre peninsula which we were visiting on an Argyll tour. Probably the only time I had the party combing a graveyard. Later that day we learned of the disastrous helicopter crash very near to where we had been.

I was never taken up on an offer I made towards the end of every tour to stop over for a few further days. The return railway tickets were usually valid for a month and I could have arranged hotel accommodation at a preferential rate.

I lost count of the times when I was merely greeted with the standard Too Busy cry of the retired. Looking after grandkids, cats, dogs, ponies or scheduled to attend meetings, on committees, PCCs, various levels of local authority or U3A as attendees or lecturers... the Grey Power generation. It reminded me that I was also trying, but not very hard, to be retired.

Chapter 27

Memories

"Everyone needs his memories.
They keep the wolf of insignificance from the door."

Saul Bellow

Many of my memories which make most impact seem to involve the countryside and natural beauty in its many forms. 21 years of happy travelling with the added privilege of introducing so many appreciative people to parts of Great Britain which they hadn't thought of visiting previously creates many memories. Some lurk in the deepest recesses and pop up unexpectedly. Others are activated by circumstance.

The first, which always hits the No 1 spot on the Memory Chart is a vision of a sunny and smooth boat-crossing from Iona to Staffa. As a lifelong fan of music the Hebrides Overture by Mendelssohn was one of the first pieces of classical music which grabbed my attention. The anticipation of really visiting Fingal's Cave was almost impossible to hide from my party. On one of the few occasions when we could actually sail into the cave, the overture, quite unexpectedly, burst out from the boat's PA system. It created a moment indelibly etched in my memory. Many subsequent visits, with the friendly puffins waiting to greet us, just reinforced that first occasion.

I write this near Midsummer Day having just returned from a nostalgic visit, my 36th, to Orkney where it is still spring. A real bonus has been to re-live that beautiful season twice in many years. South. . . then way north.

Spring comes later in the Highlands and Islands and a return to that colourful season, weeks after the first flushes of colour and burgeoning growth in the South had faded, was a never-ending treat... small fields, quite carpeted with the pale yellow of primroses. Later, the glory of the *machair* of the Western Isles with its dozens of species of wild flower per square yard, against a backdrop of a turquoise green sea washing pristine white deserted beaches, never fails to amaze. In the Northern Isles these colours are repeated on the floriferous roadside verges, with flushes of orchids leading back towards ditches packed with golden Mimulus, or the eye-catching Marsh Marigolds.

Returning in the gloaming by train from Kyle of Lochalsh towards Inverness there is the briefest glimpse of a long straggling line of deer, patiently about to cross a highland stream at its shallowest point, totally ignoring the closely-passing train. Magic indeed: a vision of seconds but imprinted on the memory for ever.

Everyone visiting the Western and Northern Isles wants to see the otters which seem assiduously to avoid the protection offered by many 'Otter Crossing' road-signs. So it was a wonderful moment to find a pair gambolling in the water right beside our parked coach at Sullom Voe – tumbling over and over in the way they always seem to perform for Simon King in Shetland. These treats are generally denied to mob-handed tourists.

Something completely different but no less memorable was being in an Orkney hotel watching a televised Proms broadcast of the first performance of Peter Maxwell Davis's "Orkney Wedding and Sunrise". To those who complained about the bottle being passed round during the performance I can only say, "You've never been to an Orkney Wedding!" The following day we visited the island of Hoy – then the home of the composer and setting for the music. Memory complete.

An evening of quite different but traditional music was presented to us at a Ceilidh in the Northbay Hall, Barra, where the party was charmed by the sheer musicality and uninhibited confidence of the island children performing; singing, dancing and playing their instruments from a long tradition of self-entertainment. And how can I forget the organiser's apology for failing to warn us that there was a "small charge"? 25p provided unlimited home-made cakes and sandwiches and bottomless cups of tea! Several visits to the Orkney Folk Festival served to re-inforce the captivating musicality of these northern islands. But in a country of never-ending surprises even I was totally blown away by a leading West African choir of 7 singing unaccompanied in a small village hall in the Highlands: moments to make the scalp tingle and the hairs on the back of the neck stand up.

The scene which comes to mind when Loch Ness is mentioned is an early morning ride beside the loch on which the Puffer 'Vic 32' was gently cruising north-easterly leaving an ever-spreading "V" of ripples on the otherwise totally mirror-like water. The temperature inversion above the loch, acting on the exhaust smoke, created a perfectly horizontal thin smoke trail forming over many hundreds of yards behind the boat ... one of the best photographs which I never took.

Only two tours evoke memories for the wrong reasons. A coach tour to the Floriade Garden Festival in Amsterdam featured traffic jams all the way to and from the port of Rotterdam to the venue at Schiphol, along with non-stop torrential rain throughout. That was one to write off as a total loss and a great disappointment to the passengers. The final scene is Mallaig, wreathed in a fog which even the gale force winds couldn't disperse. With all ferries cancelled our passages to the Small Isles of Canna, Muck, Eigg and Rum were impossible. The alternatives, from a base in Mallaig, are severely limited.

There could be a bookfull of memories of our many long holidays in Australia. Just two at this time – the surprising sight of mauve grid squares when coming over urban Brisbane before landing – the realisation – avenues of Jacaranda trees in flower – wow! The other: the many wonderful, generous, friendly people we have met there.

And finally I recall one day of a holiday on the west coast of Mull. I had a streaming cold so was unable to accompany my wife as she left on the minor ferry to explore the isle of

Ulva towards Gometra. I parked the car on a headland looking out over the islands on a day of near-perfect weather and fiddled with the car radio when I tired of hours of reading. The announcement of one of my all-time favourite pieces of music transformed me out of my lethargy as I listened to a wonderful Mahler 5 against a background of coastal beauty. That music never fails to transport me straight back there.

Chapter 28

We Discover Australia!

In 1986 on one of our last Greek Island holidays we formed a close friendship with a young Australian family on their long-service leave to whom we admitted that we would love to visit their country; then left the idea on our back-burner.

Not too long after, we received a phone call from them back in Melbourne making us a wonderful offer (family motto: *Never refuse a good offer*). Ted was in the garage business and offered to buy a campervan on our behalf – cost to us Nil! After we had seen a bit of Oz he would sell the vehicle and make a few Aussie dollars for himself. This, coinciding with a small legacy which would pay one airfare, we really couldn't refuse.

Having fallen in love with Greece we were told that the only city in the world with more Greeks than Melbourne is Athens. This overrode any residual doubts we might have entertained, although truth to tell we didn't have any.

Our first holiday there was an overwhelming success. After a quick look at Western Australia we flew on to Adelaide to meet an ex-colleague from Home Office days who escorted us around what was to become our favourite Down Under city. As South Australia's Police Commissioner he knew the area well. In a hired car (can you drive an automatic?) we gently wombled our way across South Australia to Victoria to meet our camper and Ted in Melbourne. After a few days more days' acclimatisation (splendidly hot – in January), and familiarisation with our VW Kombi we took off for our first extended exploration, over the Great Dividing Range toward the East coast in Victoria, New South Wales and Queensland. In Brisbane we left our VW under a friend's large mango tree and took a side trip to New Zealand.

The highlights of our visit to NZ were long rail journeys from Auckland to Wellington on North Island, then Picton to Christchurch on South Island. Not to be missed by any visitor to South Island is the spectacular rail journey across South Island from Christchurch to Greymouth.

Our visit to NZ was cut short by a complete inability to secure a hire car in Christchurch as the US Marines, who bravely defended New Zealand in WWII, were paying a nostalgic visit and had cleaned up all the wheels.

We also discovered what comes from "long white clouds" – long wet rain, and lots of it.

So without too much disappointment we returned early to Brisbane, collected the camper and headed further north for an unplanned visit to the Great Barrier Reef.

To say that we were totally overwhelmed by Australia, the vast distances, the deserts and beaches, but most of all the warm and friendly welcome from every Australian we met, would be an understatement. We started the holiday knowing two Australians – we finished knowing many more. And avoiding UK winters appeared not a bad idea either.

So, on returning to Melbourne we gently asked Ted if he could hang on to the van for another visit by us. This raised a slight problem in that Ted's investment and possible profit was the next term's school fees for the kids. We reached a compromise – we bought half the vehicle!

Fired up with the possibility of some really long-distance travel the following year we drove right across the vast continent, across the Nullarbor desert from East to West, a 3 ½ thousand kilometre drive, to Western Australia then up the west coast via Monkey Mia, to touch the wild dolphins, and onwards to the beautiful unspoiled Coral Bay on the Ningaloo Reef towards Exmouth. We re-crossed Australia on the Indian Pacific train out of Perth with our Kombi visible on a flat truck at the end of 30 or so coaches as we rounded the rare corners on that journey. For an encore we travelled north up the Stuart Highway to Coober Pedy, dugouts and opals, before returning our trusty vehicle to Melbourne, and buying the other half.

With the VW all ours the following year's visit was an even more ambitious trip in what was proving to be an old but thoroughly reliable vehicle, albeit without the aircon now considered an imperative. We drove from Melbourne to Adelaide where we parked the vehicle on the Ghan train which then only ran as far as Alice Springs. For three weeks we toured the magnificent ranges east and west of Alice then drove north, through Arnhem Land, to Darwin. We avoided all the much-advertised crocs for which every creek displayed a warning notice, then continued west along Highway 1 – the road which circumnavigates Australia in 14,500 km – and thence via the Northern Highway to Perth via mind-blowing displays of wild flowers reaching to the horizon. Once again we and Kombi completed the circuit by train to Adelaide.

In the words of RLS, "to travel hopefully is better than to arrive." Australia offers vast travelling-hopefully opportunities. Highway One is the world's longest designated highway and we've done most of it.

At the end of our third tour the vehicle was getting a bit tired and, after negotiations, we sold it to Ted's son, Ben – well, not all of it! (You're probably ahead of me now.)

We have enjoyed a further eight long stays of 3 to 4 months in Australia and are not too abashed to say that, apart from Far North Queensland, we have seen more of their country than many Australians – on my working stays with the Pichi Richi Railway I have often been able to suggest to Australians what they shouldn't miss on their wanderings in their own country. Conversely most of them have seen much more of Europe than we have, our brief stays there confined to Germany, Austria, France and Portugal.

A real highlight for this travelling man was a holiday when I solo-backpacked much of Queensland in 1989 during which I travelled on all the long-distance rail journeys in that vast state. Later on that holiday we celebrated my 65th by hiring the unique Railmotor 'Coffee Pot' in South Australia, and rounding up a few of our Aussie pals for a short chuff down the line from Quorn in the Flinders Ranges to a splendid birthday meal.

Being passed between friends we have acquired a whole mob of Aussie pals whose open-handed friendships have so enhanced our holidays and never cease to amaze us.

I wish I had discovered that wonderful country 60 years earlier.

Chapter 29

Why I Couldn't be a Car Dealer

I was on duty in the Police Control Room – on the ground floor of a large country house – before the days when these places became a fortress. The front door was unlocked and people would occasionally wander in thinking it was a Police Station, which it wasn't, and members of the Force and their families would use the snooker table, sometimes letting us know that they were in the building. A smiling face was followed by its body round the door. "Are you the bloke who's gotta car for sale?" I was able to say, "Yes", and led him and his wife out to the 1939 Ford New Popular which I would be heartily glad to see the back of and for which I sought £50.

It had been a disastrous purchase, from a garage, and soon after acquisition large lumps of filler started dropping off the body panels. It was a PIG to start until I discovered the secret – after about 25 turns on the starting handle with the choke held out by a row of clothes pegs it would (usually) fire up on the self-starter. Touch the throttle during this procedure and you might just as well forget it for half an hour! Fortunately I had recently gone through this routine. We walked over to the car – I held my breath, turned the key, pulled the knob, and she started. "It's a good starter" he said to his wife. We had a quick tour round the block when he asked if we could call at the home of a friend, 'a Big Ford man who knew all about Fords.' Oh dear, I saw my anticipated sale disappearing. Big Ford Man wandered down his garden path, leaned on his gate, looked at the car across the footpath and said, "That looks OK!"

Driving back towards Police HQ, where I had left my colleague with the sole responsibility for a task which now takes dozens of Communication Aides, he asked if I had any more enquiries for the car. I pointed to a group of people at the door and suggested that they too might just be waiting to see the car. His wife, in the back seat, simply handed over £50 from her handbag. Amazingly the car re-started and he drove off.

I really wonder if he was ever able to start the beast again and for several days lived in expectation of a telephone call from him or his solicitor for which I had already prepared my defence of *caveat emptor*. But far greater was my regret at having sold such a rotten vehicle to a perfectly nice trusting bloke.

But that's not the end of this story. Many years later I was speaking with a newly-found friend. Ron had served with distinction as a pilot in WWII and whilst away at war placed his new car on blocks in a safe store. When he was demobbed and returned home he was astonished to find that his father had sold it, after months of badgering from a local car dealer desperate for cars to sell in that post-war dearth of new vehicles. It was the Same Car that I had bought in 1958 – ARP 21 – the worst car I ever owned.

Its predecessors had both been sold at a profit. A 1935 Austin Ruby, bought for £40, sold for £50 despite the fact that a few weeks earlier, whilst on holiday with my girlfriend in North Wales the front nearside wheel dropped off. A search of the nearby road surface revealed the missing kingpin which I banged in with a rock and which gave no trouble thereafter. I then bought the only car which I really wish I still owned: a convertible 1939 Austin Opal 2-seater tourer. I was delighted to make £25 profit on its sale for £90, as this represented nearly three weeks' salary. Its current value would be nearer the £10,000 which I paid for my last Peugeot, which is now worth almost nothing!

Thence followed ARP 21.

Deciding that we really couldn't afford to waste any more of our non-existent reserves on a car we forwent holidays for two years and saved every penny we could. That was just enough to put a deposit on a new Mini Minor in 1959 soon after they first appeared, although only the basic model at £495 – the de-luxe was £525. But that was bad news too. It was totally unreliable and cost just about every spare penny (and more) for 2 years to keep it going.

That was to be my last British car and was followed by a perfectly reliable lifetime of Volkswagens, Renaults, Peugeots, a Simca and currently a Skoda. Best of all was a very flash, bright orange Audi with Kermit-green upholstery. All of these, of course, represented a significant loss on their sale or part-exchange but had provided us with a lifetime of many hundreds of thousands of miles travelling to all corners of this country, an occasional visit to France and a memorable journey via friends in Germany to the Mozart Festival in Salzburg.

For many years my cars exhibited a distinctive cherished number (which could be a mixed blessing!) This I acquired from a friend's old Triumph motor cycle at little cost. A long time later I sold the number to a subsequent owner of the same motor cycle who was restoring it to the condition it was in when his father had bought it new. This seemed a cogent and sympathetic reason to sell but I think I regretted the decision almost straight away, the pain ameliorated by the few quid I made on its sale.

Chapter 30

Home Sweet Home, or Dreams Come True

Despite my predisposition for travelling, home has always figured highly on my list of priorities. As a young copper in a County force I was originally required, upon marriage, to occupy a police house. This was viewed as a considerable perquisite of the job at a time when any thought of owning one's own home was quite beyond most people's financial resources. It also allowed the Chief to move men around like chessmen or allow operational flexibility – depending on whether viewed from below or above. Gradually the restriction on ownership was eased and as soon as able we purchased our first home: new, 3 beds @ £2995, but with considerable apprehension about our ability to find the £41 pcm mortgage. Ever since I had encountered the designs of Frank Lloyd Wright I dreamed of owning a long, low bungalow of my own design in grounds of at least an acre. We did not get **that** for £3k, even in 1970.

Some years later I groped my way home through a pea-souper fog after playing hijack games with the SAS over a weekend. The result had been inconclusive but at the subsequent de-briefing I think we learned that our side had lost. I was met by a wife in a state of excitement, she having seen an advertisement for a building plot for sale in our village – the first to come on the market for many years. Sale of our existing home raised the price of the plot plus some additional land and we were all set to build our dream home.

We found a builder who had just completed a house for a colleague, to his complete satisfaction. He was available to continue on our project, the plans for which we had drawn up ourselves. On our south facing plot we wanted windows to be as large as possible on the south side – the planning authorities demanded them smaller. On the north side we planned small bedroom windows – they had to be bigger. A roof pitched at a slightly lower angle than usual needed sheets of printout from a consulting engineer to prove it would hold up heavy tiles. We had already drawn up a specific planting plan for the garden with botanically correct Latin names for all major trees and shrubs. The council decided that we couldn't have 'All those foreign plants!' The approval given in their common names gave us significant flexibility.

Looking to finance the building we approached several Building Societies but none of them was prepared to grant a mortgage on premises which were not designed by an architect. At that moment banks had just started lending money for mortgages. They also had fierce old men as managers. I approached mine with due deference after waiting some days for an appointment to request what, for me, seemed an astronomical sum, to be asked merely, "Will that be enough?" Was this the start of the slippery slope which was to destroy credibility in the banking industry 30 years later?

Whilst it was nowhere near Frank Lloyd Wright proportions we looked forward to seeing our new home develop so watching it grow proved enormously satisfying until a heavy early snowfall in December arrested all activity on site for two frustrating months. Only the walls had been erected and the whole building filled with deep snow.

With the spring building continued apace and all went well – until the week before we were due to move in when extra heavy rain in July collapsed the service trenches about to be backfilled along what was to be our long access drive.

Eventually we moved in, assisted by our builder's lorry, and immediately started developing our not-quite acre flower gardens and veggie patches which were to be our pride and joy, exercise and recreation for the next 22 years, and occasionally open for fundraising. We remained totally satisfied with the four bedroom bungalow we had planned, without the interference and expense of an architect, and enjoyed many happy years living and labouring there into our retirements.

The whole process had proved so straightforward that a series in a local glossy mag based on "Who needs – building societies/builders/architects?" was prompted, much to the ire of some local architects.

When garden maintenance began to pall and strains on our ageing bods began to take longer to recover we looked to move but neither of us could think of anywhere we really wanted to move to – particularly for me, having spent all my life with my roots deeply in Northamptonshire.

The question was answered for us by the serious illness of my elder daughter who was going to need long-term support. We were extremely lucky to find a bungalow we liked near to her home and little family, and suspect we will remain here until the call to the Big Granny Farm in the sky. Our new home had been designed to totally different parameters from its predecessor but after nearly 10 years we are becoming accustomed to its differences and very grateful for its much smaller garden.

We also discovered just how many thousand miles per year we had incurred when we lived 5, 6 or 7 miles (depending which estate agent you ask!) away from our main shops, work and friends.

Chapter 31

And For Those Still Wondering

Yes, Mary left the cruise boat on the Rhine with all her teeth —
real and otherwise.

The Tour Manager's handy multi-tool and lessons learned
from a previous instant course in DIY came in handy, again,
having successfully recovered an expensive engagement ring
from a similar situation.

I had to wait until almost my last tour for what I had been
expecting to happen almost from my first: A lost return
railway ticket. 'The General' lost his return from Inverness. I
managed to talk him through to Kings Cross, from there to
Warminster he was on his own but I have no doubt that he
coped.

Approaching my 80th year life's journey continues but I
have never lost the thrill of travelling, by almost any means. I
have been privileged to be enabled to share that enjoyment.

The travel wish list grows longer — the years fewer. Who
knows with any certainty where this journey will end?

Appendix

Inspired to Visit

The islands I have been to, and other places in no particular order – many of which I probably would not have visited other than with tours, or was encouraged to explore whilst I was near:

Channel Islands
Guernsey
Herm
Sark

Isles of Scilly
St Mary's
St Martin's
Samson
St Agnes
Gugh
Bryher
Tresco

Western Isles
St Kilda
Lewis
Harris
Berneray
North Uist
Grimsay
Benbecula
South Uist
Eriskay
Barra

Vatersay
Mingulay

Shetland
Mainland
Noss
Bressay
Yell
Unst
Fetlar
Mousa
Papa Stour

Orkney
Mainland
Rousay
Papa Westray
North Ronaldsay
Hoy

Inner Hebrides
Skye
Mull
Iona
Gigha
Staffa
Easdale
Eigg
Seill
Arran
Lismore
Kerrera
Handa

Knoydart
Fair Isle
Isle and Calf of Man
Isle of Wight

Republic of Ireland
Aran Killarney and Galway
Tours took me to many more places, some now forgotten, in all parts of Scotland, Mid and North Wales and the Lake District, not to mention cruises along the Rhine and Moselle, and Eurostar day trips to Paris, Bruges and Brussels.